"Passion and Purpose. Two words that resonate deeply with me and my love for the church. But this commitment and belief in the church is shared with amazing people like Pastor Jimmy Seibert. His endurance and loyalty to the local church has opened the door for many to hear the gospel, receive salvation, and be empowered to impact their community, both locally and globally. My prayer is that his words equip and empower you to change the world through the power of the gospel."

— **Christine Caine,** *Hillsong Church, Australia, and Founder,*
The A21 Campaign

"Living for Christ with passion and purpose is truly an adventure, and there has never been a more exciting time to be a part of His story. Jimmy Seibert and Antioch Community Church have been right in the middle of this. You will be inspired by their story and how they have seen God at work in their community and around the world. My prayer is that you will carefully read this book with an eye on how it can point you toward pursuing Christ and His purposes more each day."

— **David Wills,** *President, National Christian Foundation*

"At a time when many churches have become ingrown and are struggling for survival, Antioch Community Church has discovered the key to relevance and spiritual vitality. Reflecting the New Testament principle that the local body of Christ exists to reach the nations, Antioch is effectively mobilizing and discpling believers to impact a lost world for the glory of God. Hundreds of Antioch missionaries are engaging unreached people groups around the world; the Antioch movement has spawned dozens of church plants throughout the United States, primarily among university communities, replicating the evangelizing, discipling, sending paradigm that represents the cutting edge for fulfilling the Great Commission."

— **Jerry Rankin**, *President Emeritus, International Mission Board, Southern Baptist Convention*

"Antioch is built on a foundation of godly character, skilled competence, and clear strategy to ignite movements of disciples making disciples of Jesus among the least reached people of our world. Antioch goes around the corner and around the globe to serve the least and the lost. I have witnessed the impact of their ministries for many years in many countries, and I highly commend them to you."

— **Floyd McClung**, *Director, All Nations, Cape Town, South Africa, and Author*

PASSION & PURPOSE

PASSION & PURPOSE

BELIEVING THE CHURCH CAN
STILL CHANGE THE WORLD

JIMMYSEIBERT

CLEARDAY

PASSION & PURPOSE

Published by Clear Day Publishing, a division of Clear Day Media Group LLC, Brentwood, TN. cleardaypublishing.com.

Published in association with Lux Creative {theluxcreative.com}

Unless otherwise noted, Scripture quotations are taken from the New American Standard Bible®, Copyright © 1960, 1962, 1963, 1968, 1971, 1972, 1973, 1975, 1977, 1995 by The Lockman Foundation. Used by permission. (www.Lockman.org)

Quotations designated NIV are from The Holy Bible, New International Version®, NIV® Copyright © 1973, 1978, 1984, 2011 by Biblica, Inc.® Used by permission. All rights reserved worldwide.

Quotations designated NKJV are taken from the New King James Version®. Copyright © 1982 by Thomas Nelson, Inc. Used by permission. All rights reserved.

Quotations designated ESV are taken from The Holy Bible, English Standard Version® (ESV®) Copyright © 2001 by Crossway, a publishing ministry of Good News Publishers. All rights reserved. ESV Text Edition: 2011

ISBN: 978-0-9897277-0-9

Cover Design: Kyle Rogers
Interior Design: Lux Creative {theluxcreative.com}

Printed in the United States of America.

TO MY FAITHFUL, LOYAL, AND BEAUTIFUL WIFE, LAURA,
AND TO EACH OF MY KIDS:

Abby, my daughter, and my son-in-law, Kyle
Lauren, my daughter
Caleb and Daniel, my sons

Your faithfulness to the King and His Kingdom makes it all worth it.

AND TO THE WHOLE ANTIOCH FAMILY WORLDWIDE,
WE ARE WHO WE ARE BECAUSE OF YOU.

CONTENTS

Foreword by Max Lucado *i*

Introduction *iii*

Prologue *v*

CHAPTERS

1. Being the Church 1
2. Called to Him 13
3. Life-Changing Adventure 27
4. Culture Shock and Commitment 37
5. Just Do What's Next 47
6. Miracles in the Nations 57
7. Why College Students? 69
8. Revival from the Inside Out 81
9. Dream Your Dreams 89
10. Three Church Plants 97
11. Antioch Becomes a Church 111
12. From Prison to Praise 121
13. Intentional Church 131
14. Restoration Village 143
15. The Next Twenty Years 153
16. Trusting God More 161
17. Transformation in Spheres of Society 169
18. Called to Our Nation 179
19. Reaching a Nation in Shock 185
20. Breakthrough in the Muslim World 193
21. The Passion & Purpose of Jesus 203

Epilogue *208*

Acknowledgements *210*

Antioch Churches *212*

About the Author *214*

FOREWORD

The Christian calendar is marked by three decisive days. Christmas, Easter, and Pentecost. Christmas and Easter happened outside the city, in an obscure manger, on a lonely cross. Pentecost, however, erupted in the crowded center of the city, in an international melting pot, during its most cosmopolitan moment.

In the first two events (incarnation and salvation), God worked independently, apart from people. Jesus needed no help for His birth or assistance with His death. But in the last event (proclamation), He worked through people.

They "began to speak with other tongues, as the Spirit gave them utterance. And there were dwelling in Jerusalem Jews, devout men, from every nation under heaven. And when this sound occurred, the multitude came together, and were confused, because everyone heard them speak in his own language. They were all amazed and marveled, saying to one another, 'Look, are not all these who speak Galileans? And how is it that we hear, each in our own language in which we were born? Parthians and Medes and Elamites, those dwelling in Mesopotamia, Judea and Cappadocia, Pontus and Asia, Phrygia and Pamphylia, Egypt and the parts of Libya adjoining Cyrene, visitors from Rome, both Jews and proselytes, Cretans and Arabs—we hear them speaking in our own tongues the wonderful works of God.' So they were all amazed and perplexed, saying to one another, 'Whatever could this mean?'" (Acts 2:4-12, NKJV).

The upper room prayer service became an outdoor revival. A single language became fifteen languages. Simple, uncultured, uneducated Galileans became cross-cultural communicators. Foreigners from Crete, Rome, Arabia, and a dozen other countries heard about God's wonders in their native tongues.

God's plan has not changed. He still calls common people to the uncommon task of proclaiming the gospel. God advances His church through extraordinary empowerment.

Jimmy Seibert understands this. As much as any person I know, Jimmy comprehends the powerful opportunity of our generation. He has inspired thousands of us to believe in the possibility of another Pentecost, an outbreak of hope and grace on this weary planet. Jimmy roots his convictions in the power of the gospel and the courier system of the church. His message is simple, strategy comprehensible, and evidence undeniable.

Thank you, Jimmy, for this valuable resource. Thank you, Antioch Movement, for your sacrificial demonstration. May God lead all of us into the center of our own Jerusalems, into the midst of the people. May He position us squarely in the maelstrom of cultures and languages and nations.

Do it again, Lord. Do it again.

Max Lucado
Author, pastor, minister, and dad

INTRODUCTION

This gospel of the kingdom shall be preached in the whole world as a testimony to all the nations, and then the end will come.

MATTHEW 24:14

As far back as I can remember, I was a dreamer. As a kid, I used to imagine myself throwing that winning touchdown pass to win the Super Bowl. Sometimes I was the one catching the pass. With just seconds left on the clock, I would jump up and grab the ball before landing over the goal line. The cheers were deafening as my teammates lifted me onto their shoulders.

Even as a kid, I wanted to be about something big—something much bigger than myself. I think we're actually made that way—all of us. God created us with a desire to be a part of a big story, something bigger than ourselves, something that can change the world.

Out of His mercy, God got my attention as a teenager and brought me to Himself. Little did I know the decision to follow Jesus would pull me into the greatest story of all time—God's story. And little did I know that God had a part for me to play in that story. In fact, He has a part for each of us to play. This dream was for everyone. This dream was for a people He would call His church.

Years ago, God brought together a group of people who would become Antioch Community Church. From the beginning it has been part of a God-sized story. When God was first gathering us and establishing His work in our midst, I asked, "Who are we? How do I describe what You are doing among us?" During a time of prayer, He answered with a phrase: *a passion for Jesus and His purposes in the earth.*

Yes! That is who we are. God has called us to be a people who passionately pursue Him with all our hearts and are deeply committed to His purposes. Nothing more. Nothing less.

Over the past twenty-six years, we have been on mission to love Jesus and His people and to see a lost and dying world come to know Him. About six years ago I tried to capture those first twenty years in a book called *The Church Can Change the World*. Two years later I had the opportunity to coauthor a book with Larry Kreider titled *The 3 Loves*. These books captured our history and explained the basic values by which we lived. Over the past couple of years, we have prayed about doing a new project. We wanted to take the best of what was written from the past and add our last six years, which has produced some of the most dynamic spiritual fruit we could have ever imagined. We have captured the essence of that in *Passion & Purpose*.

This book is about Antioch Community Church and its people serving around the world—a people who have been on a journey to live out God's plan by pursuing Him passionately and being committed to His purposes so everyone might have the opportunity to hear the gospel, no matter the cost. It is our story through my eyes.

Each of us has been invited into the greatest story of all time—God's story. The story of the whole world knowing His love, forgiveness, and transformation through Jesus and His church. It's not a matter of whether He is going to do it. The question is whether you and I will choose to be involved.

A passion for Jesus and His purposes in the earth. This simple phrase lived out day by day through His people can, and does, change the world.

PROLOGUE

On December 14, 2001, I was leaving my office. It had been a weary, exhausting day, and all I could think about was getting home. Those thoughts quickly changed when a reporter from the national CBS affiliate threw open the front office door and charged in. He pointed his camera straight at me and demanded, "I want an interview now! What is your response?"

"My response to what?" I asked.

"The girls were released from prison. All the foreigners have been found and are being flown to Pakistan right now!"

I was caught off guard. *What? Wait. I need to make sure this is for real.* It had been 104 days—104 very long days. Two young missionaries had been sent out from our church to serve in Afghanistan, and the Taliban arrested them. During their detainment in a harsh Afghan prison, the tragic events of 9/11 shocked the world. The United States struck back with a vengeance in Afghanistan, and our missionaries were caught in the middle.

Over those hundred-plus days, this growing church we had planted a couple of years earlier learned to pray and to love like never before. Dayna Curry and Heather Mercer, the two young women in Afghanistan, had come up through our college ministry. They were discipled in the basic values of the Kingdom of God. They learned to seek God every day, to invest in others, and to mirror God's heart for the world around them. That had led each of them to join our team in Afghanistan. Our team leaders there, along with their teammates, had also been raised up through the college ministry. During their years in Waco, they prayed consistently, "God give us a nation so we can see Your church established among those who have never heard." God replied with three simple words: *Go to Afghanistan.* And they did.

With the reporter waiting in the office, a small group of us gathered around a television. We heard Dan Rather from *CBS Evening News* confirm what we had been waiting to hear. It was true. U.S. Special Forces had landed and rescued Heather and Dayna and six other foreign-aid workers who had also been imprisoned. They were on their way home. We would find out later that the dramatic rescue was nothing short of miraculous.

I asked my assistant to call our small group leaders to get the word out. Our prayers had been answered, and we would gather to celebrate in the auditorium. Later, as I walked into that room, hundreds of people were streaming in. There were many tears and much rejoicing over the long-awaited freedom of their friends. As I looked around, I also watched as more than a hundred members of the press, from every major news agency, flocked in to get interviews. They may have come just to get a story, but they captured what God had done and was doing in our midst.

What an incredible night to be able to share the gospel with the world! The prayers of God's people, both through our church and the church at large, could set prisoners free—and they could make a way for the nations to hear the gospel.

I left the building around eleven o'clock that night, and reporters were still standing all over the parking lot. I realized that God was fulfilling His dreams through us. We had prayed, "God, would You show us how to do church so that it reproduces itself anywhere in the world? Will You give us that passion and purpose, those values that can sustain us whether in prison or the corporate world?"

And I found myself believing that the church really can still change the world.

CHAPTER 1

BEING THE CHURCH

...You shall love your neighbor as yourself...

MARK 12:31

When we started Antioch Community Church in 1999, we began to renovate an old grocery store building that had been empty for ten years. It was a revealing picture of the problems of that neighborhood—homeless men and prostitutes lived inside, and the roof was falling in. It was in the middle of a neighborhood with one of the highest rates of crime and poverty in our city at the time. Drug use and prostitution were rampant, and few businesses would locate there. The number of families living below the poverty line was far above average.

We were reaching out to people from all over our city, but our commitment to the inner city had to be at the forefront. We were called to be a multi-racial, multi-economic church, and we knew if we didn't position ourselves there, it would never happen. We also knew that if God had called us to be a people with a passion for Jesus and His purposes in all the earth, then it needed to start at home. So we intentionally moved our church building and offices into that neighborhood in Waco, Texas.

After we restored the auditorium part of the building and moved in during December 2000, Waco's city manager asked if we would host a meeting of churches interested in helping with local community development.

"I've done the math," she started. "There are more than two hundred churches in Waco proper. If each of you took four square blocks and actually loved your neighbors as yourselves, then we could take care of almost every social issue in our city. But because you won't do it, we have to do meetings like this to come up with committees and other solutions to solve the problems."

She was direct, maybe even harsh, but she wasn't wrong. Always up for a challenge, I thought to myself, *Oh, yeah, there are great churches in this city, and Antioch will join with them to see real change in Waco.*

Moving in to Make a Difference

In response to the challenge to love our neighbors as ourselves, we marked off an area of 450 homes in a nine-by-nine block area we would serve. Not only did we place the church building and offices in the inner city, but today more than a hundred people from Antioch also call the neighborhood home.

As we moved in, we saw great needs, but we weren't quite sure where to start. Plenty of experts would say we should have started a program or secured grant funding to meet the needs. As we prayed, though, we were convinced that we needed to start by simply loving and living among our neighbors. We would love our neighbor as ourselves. We would learn about their real needs without making assumptions about what those needs were. We would walk alongside our neighbors as friends and figure it out from there.

We put a moratorium on formal programming for two years. We encouraged people to start small groups, which we called Lifegroups, for prayer, Bible study, and community in their homes. We also encouraged people to start kids' Bible clubs in their front yards. But we would not create programs to meet practical needs. When someone in a Lifegroup mentioned a specific need, the group would pray about it and provide in ways that seemed appropriate. For two years we got to know our neighbors not as projects or people to fix but as friends. In that process, we learned as much from them as they did from us, and we worked together to meet the needs we saw.

Large-scale change didn't take place over night, but little by little and person by person, God used us to change lives and transform a neighborhood. In 2013, a graduate student studying social work conducted a formal survey on the impact of our church in the community. The results of that study, plus previous surveys, confirmed what we had heard from friends and neighbors: both violent and non-violent crimes decreased significantly, prostitution went from rampant to almost non-existent, student performance in the local elementary school went up, and test scores jumped significantly. Property values and home ownership increased, and neighbors expressed respect for the church's presence and work in our neighborhood.

We didn't set out with a plan to systematically change the circumstances in the neighborhood. We did set out to listen to God and to do the things He asked us to do. We asked God to open our ears and eyes to the needs around us and to what He wanted to do both in and through us.

The Feast

It didn't take long at all to notice that many neighbors were unable to meet their basic need for food. Many people were homeless, out of work, or both, so they struggled to make it day to day. In response, we began a community meal on Friday nights and called it The Feast. More than a soup kitchen to provide food, The Feast was a way to build relationships, talk about Jesus, break into small groups, and see discipleship happen. Real transformation would require intentional investment in people's lives. God was using love and meals as a doorway.

One of our leaders, Travis, started investing in a man named Branch, who started coming to The Feast each Friday with his wife, Edna, and their children. They had been homeless for almost two years, mainly because of Branch's struggle with drugs and alcohol. They were not receiving any government assistance, so they went to the different meals offered by faith-based organizations or churches to get food. Although they had claimed Jesus as their Savior, they didn't claim to be committed in their walk with Him. According to Branch, he just wasn't willing to give up that much control.

After coming to The Feast for a while, Branch realized his true need for Jesus and saw people who were willing to walk with him. He fully committed his life to Jesus, and God began to deal with him on both internal and external issues. As a church, we were able very early on to help Branch find a job and then walk alongside him as he learned what it meant to work diligently. Soon he and his family were able to move into a home, and we were able to help the kids with the tutoring they needed to be successful in school.

Branch and Edna began to attend a Lifegroup, and they brought their friends and family. Many of them came to know Jesus. Within a few short months, Branch and Edna were leading a Lifegroup, and they even helped begin three others. Eventually, their kids gave their lives to Jesus and were baptized. Over the next few months, seventeen immediate and extended family members gave their lives to Jesus. Branch, Edna, and their kids are now core members of our church. He has been on mission trips with us around the world, serving practically with his carpentry skills. Whenever I see Branch or Edna or their family, a big smile spreads across my face because they are givers as much as anyone in our congregation, both with their resources and their lives.

It all began because a hungry man needed food and found Jesus in the process.

Engaging in Education

Provident Heights is the main elementary school in our neighborhood. When we moved in, ninety percent of the 500 children it served lived below the poverty line, and overall student performance was low. Our desire was to see that change. One of our church members had become the school's principal, so we began to talk with him about how we could help.

The Texas Department of Family and Protective Services said that our neighborhood had one of the highest poverty rates among children in the entire state of Texas. We knew we had to address the issue of education if we wanted to break this cycle. One of the alarming statistics we learned is that if a child does not learn to read at grade level by third grade, there is a ninety percent chance he or she will not graduate from high school. If someone does not graduate from high school, there is a ninety percent chance he or she will be incarcerated at some point in life, if not for the majority of life. If students do not graduate from high school, they are ten times more likely to experience teen pregnancy and the related cycles that have made poverty so debilitating through the years. I could go on with the numbers, but obviously you get the point. It matters that kids are educated and cared for in their developmental years. If the family structure is not stable, then we as the church need to step in.

So step in we did. We started a program called STARS where children could come after school for help with homework and mentoring in life skills. It was simple, but the impact was profound. One of the teachers from the school wrote this letter to illustrate the way lives have been changing:

> Last year as a teacher at Provident Heights, I noticed a little boy who had transferred in from another school. He was small and wiggly and had an all too familiar wild look in his eyes. To say he got in trouble at least five times a day is not an exaggeration. Everyone was at wit's end, and we were only in the second month of school. He was two grade levels behind in reading—and every other subject for that matter. Then the teachers began to notice slight changes in him as the year continued. He wasn't getting into trouble as frequently, and his grades were improving slowly but surely. He started applying himself at school and wasn't bullying the other kids or starting fights.
>
> This gradual improvement continued throughout the school year until one day I realized this little boy hadn't been getting in trouble at all. I also noticed that he even started mediating conflicts between other children, and his grades and reading level improved

*so much that he was one of the top students in his class. He became
an avid reader and one of the most dependable and trustworthy
kids in the school.*

*Transformation had occurred. He'd become a model student.
It wasn't until the end of the school year that we discovered a man
through STARS had been mentoring him. His aunt was meeting
with a woman at church, and his family started attending The
Feast. That mentor relationship, along with outreach to his family
by other people from the church, had helped this little boy so much
that he was a completely different child at the end of the school
year. He helped his friends and worked hard at school. His attitude
improved, his grades improved, and he was a role model for the rest
of the kids in the school. Now his family and extended family are
members of the church and have come to Jesus, been baptized, and
are being transformed in the journey.*

Every week, as many as a hundred of our people are tutoring and mentoring students at Provident Heights. We have seen test scores go up and kids and their families experience the love and grace of Jesus. There are people mentoring them week by week. In one year this school went from the bottom of the rankings to achieving the second highest test scores in the community.

Crossing Language Barriers

Our inner-city neighborhood was a third Hispanic, a third Caucasian, and a third African American. Among our Hispanic friends, we discovered that many did not speak English at all, let alone as a second language. From that group, we began to deal with the complexities of various circumstances by helping people find jobs, deal with immigration issues, and face struggles with addictions. Despite language barriers, we could be engaged in people's lives. And through our desire to go to the nations, God was bringing the nations to us.

Kevin and Stacy Johnson initiated a friendship with one of their neighbors, Emily. She began to open up her heart, life, and home. Through her relationships with friends and family, more than twenty-five people either gave or rededicated their lives to the Lord. Another one of our leaders and his family also started a second Lifegroup in the neighborhood for those who do not speak English. Through those relationships the door opened to many more as we discovered more than forty people were related to this one family. As we got to know them and other friends in the neighborhood, we realized there was a need both for Spanish-speaking Lifegroups and translated worship services. A group of great leaders emerged in our Spanish ministry, and today we not only have Spanish-speaking Lifegroups, but we also have a Spanish-speaking service we simply call "Antioch en Español." Our Hispanic friends became brothers and sisters to walk with in this incredible journey together.

Mercy House

In listening to and walking alongside our neighbors, we found that many had family members and friends who were addicted to drugs. In response, we opened Mercy House in 2005. This year-long residential substance-abuse recovery program requires each resident to go through a biblically based twelve-step program, be involved in community-service projects, and receive teaching, counseling, and mentoring in both one-on-one and group settings.

One of the most powerful testimonies to come out of Mercy House belongs to Wes. For thirty-four years, Wes's use of drugs had destroyed relationships, caused him to lose jobs, and almost killed him. Ruth, Wes's sister and my administrative assistant for eleven years, was a woman of prayer who interceded for Wes consistently for years. When Ruth died of cancer, Wes took it hard. Four months after her death, he took all the drugs he had in one shot, knowing it would either kill him or scare him enough to make a change.

God saved Wes's life that day. He went to church soon after that, and there he encountered Jesus. Wes explained that during the prayer time and altar call, he felt something like warm water pouring over him, and his desire for drugs was gone. Wes bought into the idea of transformation and moved into Mercy House. Little by little, through time with Jesus, counseling, and serving others, Wes became a stronger man.

Wes's decision to follow Jesus became consuming. Before long, he began to open his heart to the nations of the world. As he prayed, the Lord would speak the word China to his heart over and over. His desire to serve in China grew, and later that year he went there on a short-term mission team.

Kandy, who was already living in China, served as the guide for Wes's team. Kandy and Wes shared a similar background. She had abused alcohol and drugs until God saved her at the age of forty. Eventually she moved to China to be a part of a church-planting team there.

After spending time together, Wes and Kandy knew they wanted to spend the rest of their lives together. Several months later, Wes proposed at the Great Wall of China, and these two have continued to love God and love their neighbors. God redeemed both of their pasts and brought them to a place where they could partner in service. After two years in China, Wes and Kandy moved back to Waco, where Wes now directs Mercy House, helping dozens of men find freedom from the same pain and brokenness he once experienced. Wes and Kandy's story is an amazing testimony of God's grace, power, and love for His children.

Grace House

Mercy House was so effective that our women decided to open a women's recovery home called Grace House. One of the women who came through was Brandy. At the age of fourteen, Brandy began experimenting with drugs and eventually moved to using methamphetamines and heavier narcotics. At twenty-two, she was arrested. Shame, guilt, and a broken marriage led her to overdose on prescription pills. In the emergency room she flat lined twice but pulled through. Six months later at a detox facility, someone told her about Grace House. This is how she tells her story:

God's love came upon me in waves. He began to reveal His love to me through His word and to show me He was there even in my darkest times. His love took me by the hand and walked me out of shame and into the fullness of who He is. Even during the times I made horrible decisions, I realized that Jesus was with me. The eyes of my heart were being opened. Jesus had chosen me as His own. I realized that with Him I was wanted and accepted. God sees me as His beloved, so I can't perform my way into or fall out of His grace. I learned this by living in Grace House.

Words were spoken over me, that I would one day have an impact on the lives of women who are walking in darkness. Isaiah 42:16 says, "I will lead the blind by a way they do not know, in paths they do not know I will guide them. I will make darkness into light before them and rugged places into plains. These are the things I will do, and I will not leave them undone." This is exactly what God has done in my life. I can see the truth with God and other people in my life. I listen to God, and I listen to people I walk with. I walk with others so I can be held accountable. And I walk with God because I have tasted the goodness of His love, and He has set my heart free.

I now live in Grace House again, but this time as a leader. Jesus has put it in my heart to live with and love women who have been hurt through their life experiences. It is my desire to take a journey with God so that other women will have a chance to know Him and His unfailing love. I want them to encounter a love so overwhelming that it takes away the heartache and pain of the past. It is the heart of God to have them walk in their true identity—to walk in the beauty of the person God created them to be and to believe and know that they really are daughters of the Most High King.

Engaging Our Community

Over the years we have had the joy of doing community events to reach out in our neighborhood. We have hosted many of what we call Community Nights. These are afternoon and evening events where we open our parking lots and invite our neighbors for food, games, music, and an opportunity to get to know us, and one another, in a non-threatening environment. Everyone loves a party, and we have had such fun gathering with our neighbors on Community Nights.

During these events we also set up a prayer tent where people could bring their needs and have someone pray for them. One of our members, Sue, shares her story about the impact of Community Nights:

> I met Wanda at Community Night. My husband and I were listening to the band, and after it stopped I thought, Well, I'm here to get to know some people. So I started talking to the woman sitting behind me. I asked her if she was a member of Antioch and she said no. She also said she hadn't wanted to come that night but something had prompted her to go. During our conversation I asked her if she knew the Lord, and she replied, "I'm not sure. There are lots of things I don't understand."
>
> I asked if she wanted to be sure, and she said yes. We walked over to the prayer tent. There my friend Sherry explained things further to Wanda, and we both prayed with her to receive Jesus as her Savior.
>
> We exchanged e-mail addresses, and through e-mails Wanda poured her heart out to me. Although Wanda didn't know a lot about the Bible, she was hungry to learn about Jesus. So we started doing discipleship lessons at her house. One of the lessons was about forgiveness. Wanda had been estranged from her daughter for two years, although she was allowed to see her grandchildren. When Wanda's daughter saw such a change in her mother she wanted to have a relationship with her again and they reconciled. Wanda began to bring her grandchildren faithfully to church each week,

and I had the privilege of praying with Wanda's daughter when she rededicated her life to Jesus.

Come Together Workdays

The more the church invested in our neighbors, the more we understood the practical needs in our neighborhood. Eventually a group of our guys started what we called Come Together Workdays (CTWs). At the first Saturday workday, more than 120 Antioch volunteers came to serve our neighborhood. The vision of these workdays was to share the love of Jesus with our neighbors by serving them in tangible, practical ways. We cut their grass. We trimmed their trees. We picked up trash. As we did these hands-on activities, we believe we imparted hope and pride back into our neighborhood. That in turn increased people's belief in the potential for change in their neighborhood and in their personal lives.

CTWs would eventually turn into block-by-block workdays on the second Saturday of each month. As we tried to be the hands and feet of Jesus, we saw families encouraged, people come to the Lord and become part of the church, and a new pride and thankfulness develop for the neighborhood.

From Friends to Family

My family lived in the church neighborhood for nine and a half years. We saw the work of God all around us. Across the street sat a drug and prostitution house, and one of the women there became one of the first residents at Grace House, where she was brought back to a place of health and freedom. A couple of the drug dealers from across the street went into our Mercy House and experienced the grace of God and the transforming work of the Holy Spirit.

This window of time changed us—me, Laura, our kids, and our Antioch neighbors. We learned to live *with* people instead of ministering *to* them. Sure, we learned that they had needs, but we also had needs. We learned from and loved one another.

This became evident when we experienced our one and only break-in while living in the church neighborhood. We had gone out to spend time as a family in a neighboring city, and somewhere in the middle of the day people had broken into our home and ransacked it. They turned over every mattress, took all our clothes out of the closets, and dumped out everything found in drawers or containers. Every square inch of our house was turned upside down, and everything valuable was gone. Even heirloom and sentimental items holding personal memories were taken.

We had decided years ago that whatever we have is God's, and we knew that we were blessed for seven years living there without incidents like this. But the question remained: who would do this? Was it people from the neighborhood or people from outside the neighborhood?

The answer showed up on our doorstep later that evening. A man named Anthony knocked at the door. He was one of our Hispanic friends who had come out of drug addiction and was now part of our church family. It had been about six hours since the break-in when he stood there, tears in his eyes, to say, "I've checked around with everybody. It's nobody in the neighborhood. I wouldn't let it happen. Nobody would let it happen. You're a part of us, and we won't steal from family."

Then he said, "Here, I need to give you this," and he handed me $41 in cash.

"Anthony, I can't take that," I responded automatically. I knew his family was living day to day and many times didn't even have enough for that day.

He looked me in the eyes and said, "You have to—you're family. This is what we do."

As he walked away, I thought, *This is what it's all about—people loving people in the name of Jesus. This is the church.*

LOVING JESUS AND LOVING OUR NEIGHBOR CAN NEVER BE SEPARATED. WHEN WE LIVE THOSE TRUTHS OUT IN COMMUNITY, WHOLE NEIGHBORHOODS CAN BE TRANSFORMED.

CHAPTER 2

CALLED TO HIM

But seek first His kingdom and His righteousness,
and all these things will be added to you.

MATTHEW 6:33

When we think about what changes our lives, it always begins with our hearts. Let me take you back to where this journey began for me.

Searching for an Answer

I wonder if God is real.

I was a high school sophomore in Beaumont, Texas, when that thought kept coming back to me. I was waking up to the fact that partying, sports, and friends were not meeting the deep needs of my heart. I decided the obvious place to get my answer would be a church.

After staying out almost all night at a party on Saturday, I got up early the next morning, which was certainly not the norm. I put on slacks and a button-up shirt and drove off in search of a house of God. As far as I was concerned, anything with a steeple and stained glass windows would do. I found one, slid into the back pew, and waited for my answer.

For three Sundays in a row, I sat on the back pew in three different churches, hoping to hear something about God that would make Him real to me. But I didn't hear anyone tell me clearly how I could know God. By the third visit, I put it out of my mind and went on with life as usual. However, God had not forgotten me.

An Encounter with God

"Hey, Seibert!" Someone called my name as I walked across the parking lot after football practice. I looked over to see my friend Clint.

"Hey, man," he said. "You still coming to my house?"

"Sure," I mumbled half-heartedly. Clint had been hounding me for days about listening to some story about a guy who had "found God." Soon, we were listening to a recording of a man who chronicled a life of privilege and eventually addiction and brokenness. He said he had been transformed by the simple message of Jesus and His power to set people free and forgive any sin.

I had heard that Jesus loved people and had died on a cross, but I had honestly never heard that I could know Him personally or what it all meant. I was faced with a decision, but I didn't know what to do next.

That evening when I walked in my house, I was surprised to see my older brother, David, sitting there. He lived four hours away in Waco, where he was a student at Baylor University, so it was unusual for him to be home in the middle of the week. The timing was perfect.

David had experienced God in college, although I wasn't exactly sure what had happened to him. What I did know was he began asking to pray before meals when he was home. Of course, some of his prayers were awkward attempts to share the gospel with us. On Thanksgiving he had prayed something like this:

> *Lord Jesus, I thank You for loving us and having a perfect plan for our lives. All of us are sinners and have fallen short of Your glory, but if we repent and turn to You, Jesus, then You will save us and make us new creatures. Thank You for this family and for this food. Amen.*

Obviously David was trying to say something, but I had no idea what it was at the time. As I walked in the door that Wednesday evening, though, I was starting to put the pieces together. I skipped all the small talk and blurted out, "Hey, Dave, you've become kind of religious. I heard this story tonight about a guy who says he came to know Jesus. What do you think about that?"

David opened his mouth to answer, but then he paused. Wisely, he asked, "Well, what do you think about it?"

I wasn't sure. Somehow I realized this was a big commitment. In a moment of transparent honesty, I said, "If I do this I'll have to live differently. I don't know if I'm ready."

"Do you believe Jesus is who He says He is and that He has eternal life for us?" David asked.

"Yes."

"Then what are you waiting for?"

As those words hung in the air, I realized God was answering the question I first asked a year earlier. He was real, and He was inviting me into the divine relationship for which He had created me.

I prayed a simple prayer with my brother that night: "Lord Jesus, I need You in my life. I have sinned against You and others. I want You in my life." In that moment an incredible peace filled my heart, a peace I had never known before. And for the first time in my life, I didn't feel alone.

First Attempts

David left Beaumont the next morning, headed back to Waco. Before leaving, he gave me my first discipleship lesson.

"Read the Bible. Pray every day. And tell everyone you know about Jesus," he said.

Then he handed me a Christian music cassette (this was back in the day, after all) called *Happy Man* by B.J. Thomas. "Listen to it every day," he said as he walked out the door.

So with that crash course in discipleship, I started reading my Bible, talking to God, and attempting to share my faith. What my brother neglected to mention was that most people wouldn't exactly appreciate it when I shared my faith.

A couple of weeks after my decision to follow Jesus, I went to the beach with friends for our annual spring break getaway. We were sitting in lawn chairs at the edge of the water, fishing and drinking beer, just as we had always done. This time, though, Clint and I had agreed beforehand that we would try to share our faith. One by one, we walked around to the lawn chairs, asking our friends what they thought about God and what they knew about Jesus.

After a few minutes, the unofficial leader of our group shouted angrily, "Hey, what's your deal? Why are you trying to ruin our time by talking about God? We're just trying to have a good time here. Have you gone weird or religious or something?"

Clint and I fumbled around, said nothing, and sat in awkward silence. We were not ready for that kind of pushback. The rest of the week we backed off and went with the flow as if nothing had changed in our lives.

The rest of my junior and senior years of high school looked pretty much the same. I didn't have regular Christian community or discipleship, and I didn't grow much spiritually. My days slipped back into a normal routine. Still, I knew God was with me.

It was in the midst of that season when God spoke to me in a way I had never experienced before. One night in a dream I found myself standing in a windy wheat field. A white fence ran before me, through the middle of the field as far as I could see. I heard a voice say, "I am coming to separate the wheat from the chaff, and no longer will people be able to ride the fence. They will either be for Me or against Me."

Then I woke up. God had been speaking to me.

I had never had a spiritual dream before. I didn't know this kind of thing actually happened to people, but I was certain that God had spoken to me. Unsure of what to do about it, I simply went on with my life, but it wasn't long until that dream became significant.

The Wheel

Thud. I slammed the trunk of the car. My orange Ford Fiesta, affectionately known as The Pumpkin, was stuffed to the brim with boxes and luggage. I was headed to Waco, where I would start my freshman year at Baylor University.

I went inside to say goodbye to my parents. As final parting words, my mom said, "Remember, Jimmy, college is about more than good grades. Get to know people. Experience different things."

Absolutely! Thank you! I thought to myself. Four hours later, I was in Waco and ready to take that advice to heart.

My career ambition at that time was simply to become an influential person, whether through business, law, or politics. I chose Baylor because I had heard there were people who loved and knew Jesus, and I wanted to learn how to do that, too. I showed up on campus with both of those desires in my heart.

During freshmen orientation we were introduced to a diagram called the Welcome Week Wheel to illustrate the concept of living holistically. Picture a wheel with Christ in the middle surrounded by four spokes labeled *physical, social, spiritual,* and *intellectual.* Of course, I wanted to succeed, so I decided to dive in headfirst.

To check off the physical part, I began working out and getting in shape. To cover the spiritual spoke, I joined Bible studies and went to church every Sunday. I also made dating and hanging out top priorities. (I had to—it was a Wheel mandate!) Last, I attended to the intellectual spoke by working just hard enough to make B's and honoring that great advice my mom had given me.

Over my first two years of school, I followed the Wheel assignment faithfully. I also joined a fraternity, pursued leadership opportunities, and got involved in service projects. I wanted to find the fast track to "be somebody." Yet I came to the end of my sophomore year and still felt as though something was missing.

At a church service, I heard the phrase *riding the fence.* My dream about the wheat field came rushing back, and I realized the fence from that dream was the dividing line for following Jesus wholeheartedly. I could not live on the fence. I was either going to be for Him or against Him. Until then, my basic understanding was that God loved me no matter what, and as long as I didn't do anything super bad, I would be fine. I could pursue all my ambitions as long as I tagged on an "I'm doing all this for God" sentence at the end. Although it sounded good, I knew in my heart I couldn't continue to skirt along the fence.

I found myself praying earnestly, "God, I want to follow You with all my heart. I really do. But I need you to show me how."

A Change of Heart

At the time I was dating a girl who, like me, was a young believer. We started searching Scripture together and trying to better understand what it meant to follow Jesus. Day by day, God drew me closer to Him through His Word. My girlfriend, on the other hand, began to drift away from me.

At the end of the spring semester, I went to her home in San Antonio for a few days. Just hours into my time there, my girlfriend and I were standing in her backyard talking when she broke the news to me that she no longer wanted to date me. I was devastated. I thought we were the perfect couple. I even thought we were heading toward marriage. I didn't understand.

After that defining conversation, I went jogging, hoping to release some of the sadness and anger I was feeling. Running down the street and crying out for help in my emotional pain, I realized I had a choice to make. I could either run *to* God in my pain or I could run *from* Him. It was as simple as that. My choice right then, as much as any other decision I've made, changed the course of my life.

The next morning, as I drove down Interstate 10 from San Antonio toward Beaumont, I made a deal with God. "I'll give you three months to show me who You really are," I prayed with my hands tightly gripping the steering wheel. It was audacious, teetering on the edge of arrogance. More than a request, it came out as a demand, but I was desperate. I needed God to reveal Himself.

Seconds after I uttered this prayer, I was suddenly aware of things in the car that were obstacles to my walk with God. Glancing at the passenger seat, I saw a half-empty pouch of Beech-Nut chewing tobacco. It had been a habit since seventh grade. I grabbed it and threw it out the car window. Next, I noticed the stack of music cassettes of bands I'd loved my whole life. One by one I also threw them out the window, leaving behind a stream of litter and distraction. I needed to get rid of anything that would keep me from pursuing God with all my heart. By the time I reached Beaumont, I had decided to give up movies and television for three months, too. When I saw actors on the screen, I often compared myself to them instead of Jesus, so I had to turn off that distraction. I gave God only three months, but I was determined to see how He would reveal Himself. If that meant stripping away things one by one so I could focus, then that's what I would do.

At home, I had a job lined up at a chemical plant eight hours a day. My daily routine for the summer would be to wake early to spend time reading the Bible and praying before heading off to work. I decided, for whatever reason, that I would start in the New Testament, read a chapter every day, and then do exactly what Jesus said to do. Unlike before, though, my prayers didn't stop when I closed my Bible. I found myself talking to God throughout the day, asking for help as I tried to live out whatever I could remember from the words I'd read that morning. Turns out, doing exactly what the Bible says is a lot harder than it sounds.

By the end of Matthew 6, I had given away almost everything I owned and had forgiven people I had not planned on forgiving. By the time I made it through the entire book of Matthew, my worldview had been flipped upside down.

I remember simply talking to Jesus like a friend as I shuffled papers at the plant, day in and day out. Each day brought us closer, filling me with the peace and fulfillment I'd been craving. It was as though He was walking right next to me, through both ups and downs. Through the mundane and the exciting, He was a constant presence.

Somewhere in the middle of the summer, I thought, *Man, I'm turning into a weirdo! All I do is read the Bible and pray.* But the more I thought about it, the more I realized I had never before sensed God's presence, love, and peace like I was experiencing them then. *Oh well,* I concluded, *if that's what a weirdo is, then that's okay with me. I want to be wholly His—I need to be wholly His.*

My three-month bargain ended in the middle of August, and my life had changed. I had changed. The morning I had planned to return to Baylor, I woke up at 6:00 a.m. As I sat down to read my Bible, tears began to fill my eyes. *What's going on?* I wondered as I wiped them dry. But by the time I got in the shower, a trickle of tears had turned into sobbing. I had never been an especially emotional person, so I couldn't understand why I was weeping uncontrollably. At the breakfast table, the tears kept coming. My parents stared at me with looks of obvious concern.

"What's wrong with you?" my father asked.

"You're falling apart. Do we need to get you a psychologist?" my mom offered.

"Son, have you taken this religious thing too far?" my father added.

I didn't actually know why I was crying. I finally got out, "No, I just love you guys. That's all it is."

Somehow I managed to convince them of my sanity, and they reluctantly let me leave for Waco. Then I continued to cry for two hours on the road.

"What is wrong with me?" I cried out to God.

He spoke to my heart: *You asked me to show you I'm real, and I have come.* In that moment, I realized every question I had asked, God had answered. God's Kingdom had become real, and I was forever changed.

A Different College Experience

Because I had changed so much over the summer, my last two years at Baylor looked remarkably different than the first two. When I got back to Waco, I discovered I wasn't the only one who'd had a powerful encounter with Jesus over the summer. I began getting together with a group of guys in the evenings, and God would meet us as we worshipped, prayed, confessed our sins, and shared our lives with one another. I started to understand what the New Testament Church experienced as they met house to house (Acts 2:42-47).

One day after class my roommate, Ben, and I were hanging out at our apartment, and we decided to pray together. As we were on our knees, seeking the

Lord, I kept seeing a picture in my mind. Jesus was walking down the middle of a road. Along each side of the road people were standing in ditches. It seemed as though I was supposed to be walking down the middle with Jesus. I told Ben what I had seen, and he said he was seeing the same image as he prayed.

As we began to talk about it, we realized the image had to do with a common debate in the church at that time regarding conservative versus charismatic theology and expression. We felt Jesus was telling us that some people had fallen into various rigid camps, but if we would just follow Him, we would always be on the right path. That experience marked both of us. We learned we were never to get caught up in controversy, but simply to follow Jesus and His Word.

A Heart for the Nations

"Have you ever heard of missions?"

I was out for a bike ride with my buddy Kyle when he threw out this question.

"No. What is it?" I asked.

"Missions is where you go to other nations to tell people about Jesus," he explained.

"That sounds great. Do you know anybody who knows anything about it?"

"No. Why don't we pray and ask God to show us?" Kyle suggested.

The next morning we went to Sunday school at Highland Baptist Church with some friends. It was announced that a missionary from Thailand would be giving a talk titled "What Is Missions?" in one of the classes that morning. Kyle and I looked at each other and stood up to find the class.

The missionary, Dave, opened his Bible and read Matthew 28:19-20 about God's call to the church to share Jesus with the nations. With a passionate yet humble plea, he challenged us to embrace this great commission, living as Christ's ambassadors on the earth. I was impressed with his message and the way he was living out the words he read in the Bible.

After his talk, Kyle and I, along with our friends Bill and Susan, went to talk to the missionary. I wanted to affirm him. "Hey, man," I began. "I just have to say that you're doing a great job. Preaching out of Matthew like that was right on. I've been spending a lot of time in that book, and I have to say you're *really* preaching the Word. Way to go."

What Dave was thinking at that moment of my naïve arrogance I will never know. But he seemed encouraged, if not amused, by my eager affirmation. "Thanks," he said.

Then he added, "You know, I have a friend in Papua New Guinea who looks for lost tribes in the jungle who have never heard the gospel. He could always use some help. Would you be interested in working with him this summer?"

Without hesitation, three of us responded, "That would be great!"

Bill, Susan, and I went to lunch and dreamed about the adventure. Over the next few months, we saw God move powerfully as we prepared to go, and eventually we would find ourselves in the jungles of Papua New Guinea.

Preparing for the Future

Hey, she sure is good looking. I wonder if she would go to Papua New Guinea.

I saw Laura Mielke sitting in the back of a Campus Crusade meeting that fall. That night I asked my roommate Sam if he thought she would go. According to Sam, Laura loved Jesus and would probably do whatever He wanted her to do. That was good enough for me, so I asked her out and we went on our first date a few days later.

I really had changed in six months. Before, I would have asked out Laura simply because she was beautiful. After six intense months with Jesus, though, the question in my mind changed. What was more important was how much she loved Jesus. Of course, it didn't hurt that she was beautiful!

Laura and I had gone out a few times, building our friendship, before I went to a discipleship ministry in Almont, Colorado, over the Christmas break. Bob and Becky Stuplich had a vision for a ministry much like Francis Schaeffer's L'Abri in Switzerland. Francis Schaeffer had discipled Bob through challenging years in the 1960s and '70s, and Bob had come out of that experience with a desire to do the same for others.

Over those few days, we talked about the claims of Jesus and what it meant to follow Him wholeheartedly. Sitting by a crackling fire in their living room, I listened as Bob and Becky talked about their lives and how Jesus had changed and led them. I realized God was speaking to me regarding specific issues in my life. I was self-centered and impatient, and that had to change. Every day while I was there, I read 1 Corinthians 13's words about loving in a way that is patient, kind, not jealous … and endures all things—and I realized just how hard those words are to live out and how much help I needed. I prayed over and over, "God, teach me to be patient and loving." Little did I know that when you pray prayers like that, God is committed to answering them, but not always in the way you would have chosen.

Within a week of returning to school that January, I knew something was wrong with Laura. She had been at our apartment for dinner and had left to walk home when God's voice stopped me cold. *She's in trouble.* Startled, I looked around, wondering if I'd imagined it.

I told my roommate what I'd heard. He told me his cousin had anorexia nervosa and suggested Laura was exhibiting the same kind of signs. It seemed everywhere I turned the next few days, people were coming to me with concern for Laura. After a day of seeking the Lord, I knew I had to talk to her.

"Laura," I started as gently as I could, "it seems you have a problem with anorexia and need to deal with it. Whether you love me or hate me, I'm committed to stand with you as you work through it."

That night began a difficult journey for Laura and me. It was hard for her to hear my input, as she told me later. Anorexia is a control issue, so someone confronting you, forcing you to admit you have a problem, is the first step in relinquishing that control. She had fallen into the eating disorder because of her struggle with feelings of insecurity and comparing herself to others. She discovered one thing she could control was her appearance, and before long she was trapped in the pain and lies of anorexia.

Over the next several months, God broke both Laura and me as we sought

Called to Him

freedom for her from that evil stronghold. I stood by her both in prayer and at the dinner table. When we were at restaurants, I purposely ordered more food than I needed so I could say, "Look at my plate. There's not much on yours." I gained fifteen pounds, and there were times she hated me, but through it all, I stayed the course I believed God had called me to walk. And in the process I was learning both patience and that 1 Corinthians 13 kind of love.

I also learned that God is the strong one, not me. No matter how much I wanted to fix Laura's circumstances, I couldn't. But God could. My patience and love for Laura had to come out of total reliance on God. Any healing that would take place wasn't up to me.

A Spiritual Breakthrough

Around spring break of that year, I reached out to my friend Chris, who was a Christian counselor. As I told him about Laura's situation, he reminded me of an important truth: the battle was not with flesh and blood but with a spiritual enemy.

"I think you should both fast and pray for a spiritual breakthrough," he suggested.

I shook my head. "No! You're telling me she should stop eating? Starving herself is the problem."

He graciously explained the difference between spiritual fasting and simply not eating. After we talked for a while, Laura and I decided to take his advice, seeking God's power through fasting.

It didn't take long to realize I had been trying to fight a spiritual battle through physical power. I had been trying to convince Laura by using words, out-eating her at meals, and doing everything I could think of in my own strength to make her change. None of it worked. But as we cried out to God through prayer and fasting, I began to see the Spirit move in her life.

As I witnessed the change in Laura, I became increasingly aware of my own need for God's Holy Spirit. At church I saw others experiencing God's presence in a powerful way. The Holy Spirit was alive in their midst. A continuous message being preached was that God wanted to give us victory in every area of our lives.

In my desperation to see a spiritual breakthrough in both Laura's life and my own, I drove out to Lake Waco one night. As I sat in my car in the dark, I cried, "Holy Spirit, if You're real, I need You!" It wasn't a theological question but a desperate cry for God's help. I was secure in my salvation, but I knew I needed all the power God had in order to help Laura.

Somehow I knew God had heard my request. After that experience I began to believe God would meet me in my need. I read through the book of Acts, looking for places where the Holy Spirit showed up, and I asked Him to show up in the same way in my life. By the time I got to chapter 4, I noticed that the people who received the filling of the Holy Spirit in Acts 2 still needed that same filling two chapters later in order to have boldness to preach the gospel.

A couple of days later, somewhat frustrated, I went into my room and locked the door. I told God, "I won't leave this room until You have fallen on me just as You did for the people in Acts!" It was a bold move, and I meant it. I resolved to stay there until the Holy Spirit showed up in my life.

As I began to pray and worship, God did show up. An unexplainable joy bubbled up inside me, and He spoke mysteries to me that I couldn't yet understand. It was life-changing. But that outpouring of God's Spirit was not a one-time experience. It became a catalyst into daily reliance on God's power through His Spirit in everything I do.

God was working powerfully in Laura during that time as well. God had given me a specific verse for Laura's journey: "I am the LORD your God, who brought you out of Egypt so that you would no longer be slaves to the Egyptians; I broke the bars of your yoke and enabled you to walk with heads held high" (Leviticus 26:13, NIV). In other words, God gave His people freedom. I had been praying this daily for her.

Unaware that I was praying those words, Laura was praying with another friend one night when the power of God came on her. She saw in her mind an image of a little girl in a cage. God came and bent the bars of the cage, calling her out. Laura called me overjoyed. I told her the Scripture I had been praying. We knew God was creating a breakthrough.

Any authentic encounter with the Holy Spirit results in change. Laura had faithfully watched a soap opera for seven years. That very day when she tried to watch it, it made her physically sick to her stomach, and she never watched it again. At that time, she also began waking up in the middle of the night for many nights, and she journaled what God was speaking to her about His great love for her. Most people diagnosed with anorexia struggle with it their entire lives, but for Laura, the bondage was broken and she was free to move forward. Hers is a testimony of the power of God to accomplish the impossible. That experience was an early step on an incredible journey into the Kingdom of God. It was a glimpse into understanding His passion and purposes.

In a few short years, I saw how God's earlier prophecy of separating the wheat from the chaff was coming to pass in my life. God didn't want me to ride the fence. He wanted me to be completely His. I was now ready to go to the nations.

> READING THE WORDS OF JESUS AND OBEYING THEM PREPARES THE WAY FOR THE GOD-SIZED ADVENTURE WE WERE MADE FOR. ABSOLUTE SURRENDER IS OUR GATEWAY TO THE KINGDOM OF GOD.

CHAPTER 3

LIFE-CHANGING ADVENTURE

Go therefore and make disciples of all the nations ...
and lo, I am with you always, even to the end of the age.

MATTHEW 28:19-20

David Sitton was like Indiana Jones for Jesus, trekking through the mountains of Papua New Guinea to share the gospel at any cost. And during the summer between our junior and senior years of college, Bill, Susan, and I found ourselves on a wild and crazy journey with him.

On our first adventure, we drove a four-wheel-drive truck into a jungle on precariously rough, narrow roads, and then we hiked the rest of the way to the river. There, we met a couple of local men who would guide us upriver to a village of people who had never heard the gospel. The new surroundings seemed to come straight from the pages of *National Geographic*. Our new friends had bones through their noses and war paint on their bodies—something I most definitely did not see growing up in Beaumont.

As we sat in dugout canoes gliding up the Sepik River, red crocodile eyes peered at us from the water's edge, and rain began to fall. In that moment, reality hit me. The thought that raced through my mind went something like this: *What an idiot. What in the world have I gotten into? I'm going to die out here in the middle of the jungle! Stupid! Stupid! Stupid!* The feeling that went through my gut was something akin to—or maybe exactly like—panic. I held my hands as close to myself and as far from the jaws beneath those red eyes as possible.

As we continued down the tributaries that would lead to the village, the rain poured and darkness took over. I became keenly aware of our need for God. This trip was serious business, and we'd have to rely on God on a whole new level.

When we docked, several villagers extended a plank to help us get ashore. Bill and I were carrying a generator across, but when I reached the top, the plank broke in half. All six feet two inches and 230 pounds of Bill fell into that crocodile-infested river. I had never seen anyone walk on water, nor have I since, but Bill came as close as anyone. Within seconds, he was out of the water and running past me on the bank.

As we pitched our tents that night, I was wondering if it was worth it. The next morning brought the answer. Because we knew that local folklore told of a creator god and a great flood, we came prepared to share the gospel using a slide show called "Creation and the Flood." We explained that the god they had been trying to appease for years was not one of fear but one of love. We explained that He was God, and as we talked about the love of Jesus, people responded. That morning, we saw nineteen people give their hearts to the Lord. Over the ensuing days, much of the rest of the village would do so as well.

After seven days of ministry in the surrounding areas, we were preparing to leave when a man sent for us to come and pray for a man in his village. Suffering from cancer, he had lain on his mat for two months, unable to get up.

"I either want God to heal me or to let me die and end this misery," he said through a translator.

We shared the gospel with him, and he accepted Jesus as his Savior. We prayed earnestly for his healing, but nothing happened. The next morning as we were leaving, though, one of the villagers ran up to us shouting, "The old man is up! The old man is up! He is fixing breakfast for you. He has been healed!"

God was indeed alive and active in that village. And over the years since, I've come to know that He is indeed alive and active everywhere around the world.

Blackwater Fever

"I'll be back in a week."

Those were the pilot's words as he landed the bush plane on a grass airstrip in the mountains of Papua New Guinea. What great comfort they were to young missionaries heading blindly into the unknown!

David was taking us into the mountains in search of tribes who had yet to hear the gospel. We hiked in and walked from village to village, asking people if they knew of Jesus and sharing the good news of His love and salvation. Some were receptive, and others weren't. We had been going for four days when David contracted blackwater fever, a deadly complication of malaria.

His only chance of survival was to return home immediately for medical attention. The next village was expecting us, though, and it would have been seen as an insult if we broke our promise and did not go there. David suggested that Bill and I should continue to the village, and he and Susan would radio for the airplane to return the next morning. His parting words were a warning.

"You guys absolutely must return by nightfall, or you'll miss the flight off the mountain," he said. "You can't be late, and you don't want to be stuck in the jungle overnight."

Bill and I traveled on to the village with our guides. God was at work, and more people came to know Jesus. Time got away from us, though, and nightfall was fast approaching.

"There is a shortcut," the guides told us, "but it's extremely difficult. We don't think you want to take it."

"What do you mean?" we countered. "Of course we want to!"

Oh, the arrogance of youth. Bill and I took off with enthusiasm. We were young. We were strong. We were athletes. We could take this mountain.

By the time we were down just one of the mountains, the guides were carrying our backpacks. As we made our way up the next one, we were practically crawling. Those gracious guides helped us along and waited patiently during our frequent stops to catch our breath. We made it back to the village just as utter darkness took over.

"Where have you been?" Susan's voice was a mixture of concern and irritation, but mostly irritation. That was the last time I cursed publicly.

It's true that God's strength shows up in our weakness. The next morning, the plane came and we all flew back to Wewak, our base city, so David could get the medical care he needed. God was steadfastly faithful during those days in Papua New Guinea. He protected us from harm, provided for us through the kindness of the people we met, guided our steps in the dark, and strengthened us when we were at the end of ourselves. Most amazing of all, He allowed us to step into the adventure of sharing His good news and seeing the power of His Spirit move among people in even the most remote, forgotten places.

Give and It Will Be Given

It's a miracle we even made it to Papua New Guinea in the first place. Just one month before we were supposed to leave, we still needed to raise an additional three thousand dollars.

Ten months earlier, that would have been no problem. I earned more money than I ever had working at the plant in my hometown. At the same time, though, I was reading through the book of Matthew, determined to do what Jesus said, no matter what. When I got to Matthew 5:42—"Give to him who asks of you, and do not turn away from him who wants to borrow from you"—I decided I would give if anyone asked, even though it felt good to have so much money. By spring of that year, I had given away half of what I'd earned. My bank account continued to dwindle until I was broke, but I committed to believe God would take care of me when I obeyed His Word.

That commitment was tested when our college pastor told us that we needed to come up with more money to make the trip happen. A lot more money—and fast. "Well, if God told us to go, then He will provide the money," Bill declared confidently. I tried to cling to that same faith, but I wasn't so sure.

The following Wednesday night at church, I had exactly one dollar left in my wallet. Then a friend walked up and handed me twenty dollars that I had forgotten he owed me, bringing my total net worth to twenty-one dollars.

Later in the service, when the offering plate came my way, I felt God urging me to put it in. All of it. In that moment there was no logical reason to give away all my money, but a commitment to follow Jesus' lead without question was reason enough. So I put it in. All of it.

Sunday afternoon my mom called to tell me I was fifty-four dollars short on my rent that month. I wasn't sure what to do, but I held to my commitment to believe and follow Jesus. At the Sunday night service, the pastor announced he was taking an offering for people who had needs. One of the specific needs he felt God was showing him was that someone needed about fifty dollars for a rent payment.

He encouraged anyone with need to talk to the associate pastor following the service. I sat quietly. I'd never accepted money from anyone, and I wasn't about to start talking publicly about being broke. After the service, we were talking to the pastor about our upcoming trip to Papua New Guinea, and I remained silent. Soon, though, I felt convicted to put aside my pride and confess that the rent money might be for me. The pastor called the associate pastor and verified that no one had come forward for the rent money yet. A few minutes later, the associate pastor walked in the office and handed me an envelope.

"God told me the rent was fifty-four dollars," he announced, "but He also said I should give you an extra twenty-one dollars. So here's seventy-five dollars."

As we watched God's provision pour in over the following weeks, our faith grew. A few days later, a gentleman wrote a check for $2,200 toward our trip. The next day, I found a hundred-dollar bill in the tape deck of my car. We were well on our way to our goal of three thousand dollars.

The next week, when finals were over and school had ended for the semester, I sold all my books and paid all my bills. I had fourteen dollars left over. My plan was to drive to Houston to see Laura before I left for Papua New Guinea. All I had was those fourteen dollars and a quarter tank of gas, but I'd been watching God perform financial miracles, so I trusted He would find a way to get me to Houston.

A couple of days later, Susan, Bill, and I were scheduled to present our remaining financial need to our congregation at Highland Baptist Church during the Sunday evening service. It was our last shot at funding the rest of the trip to Papua New Guinea. As I stepped out of my car to walk inside, I sensed the Holy Spirit tell me, "Get your wallet."

But I have only fourteen dollars, I thought. Still, I knew it was the Spirit's voice, so I grabbed my wallet and went in to worship. When the offering plate came by me, I gave the full fourteen dollars. For the first time in my life, I stood up in worship when no one else was standing. With hands raised and tears flowing, I said, "Oh, God, I surrender all." I knew I had nothing left.

That night, Marjorie Saint, the wife of Nate Saint, one of the five famous missionaries killed among the Huaorani Indians in South America, spoke at the service. She asked people to contribute toward building water wells in Africa, where her son was currently working. Everyone responded enthusiastically, giving more than three thousand dollars collectively.

The pastor then introduced François, another missionary in the service that evening. He shared, and we took another offering to support his work in France. As the congregation sang the benediction song, I thought we were sunk. But then, as the pastor was about to dismiss the service, he remembered us.

"Wait. There are also three college students going to Papua New Guinea this summer to serve as missionaries. If anybody wants to help out, they're over there," he said, pointing in our direction.

Even through what was little more than an afterthought in promoting our need, God showed His faithfulness. The first person who walked up to us was a businessman in our church who knew that we had not yet bought our tickets, and he handed us three tickets to Los Angeles for the first leg of our trip. Others handed us cash and checks. As we rejoiced over God's provision, I opened my Bible and found two crisp hundred-dollar bills. I was amazed. When it was all said and done, we had fifteen hundred dollars more than we needed. When we talked after the service, Bill and Susan said they thought the two hundred dollars in my Bible was not for the trip but for me personally to use to see Laura in Houston before we left. Within a year of learning to "give to him who asks of you," I also learned the truth of Luke 6:38: "Give, and it will be given to you."

Several days later, as Bill, Susan, and I sat on a plane headed for Papua New Guinea, I asked the Lord for a Scripture for the summer. He led me to Matthew 28:19–20: "Go therefore and make disciples of all the nations, baptizing them in the name of the Father and the Son and the Holy Spirit, teaching them to observe all that I commanded you; and lo, I am with you always, even to the end of the age." God highlighted the last phrase for me, saying, "If you will simply go, I will always be with you." In the coming days I would discover the powerful truth of those words.

Fighting a Spirit of Fear

If David Sitton was Indiana Jones for Jesus, Fred Piepman was a mashup of the apostles Peter and Paul. After being on the mission field ten years, Fred had discipled scores of Papua New Guinean men, planted more than sixty churches, seen many healed of various diseases, and even seen people raised from the dead. God's power moved intensely in Fred's life and ministry, and people's lives were changed because of it. After spending half the summer with David, Bill and I joined Fred's ministry for the rest of our trip while Susan stayed with David and his family to serve and minister with them.

Fred believed in on-the-job training when it came to discipleship and church planting. He invested in us with words and then let us experience first-hand the realities of what he had taught. He said we would start in an area called Benna. While some regions where Fred worked were highly responsive to the gospel, the people in Benna had been aggressively resistant. The villagers had run off the last missionary by burning down his house. Apparently Fred thought this sounded like the best place to start for two college students who had never done this before.

The night before we left for Benna, we spent time praying with Fred and his wife, Darlene. As we waited for God to speak, Darlene said, "I feel we should pray for your safety."

While I appreciated the prayers, I wished she had kept that concern to herself. To say the least, I was scared to death. My fear was real and had been building. The night before, I woke up with a jolt when I felt something, or some-one, choking me. It felt as though the devil himself had his hands around my neck. After struggling with all my might, I managed to say the name of Jesus, and the choking stopped. I knew beyond a doubt that God had protected me, but I lay awake terrified the rest of the night.

After we prayed, I confessed my fear to Fred, and Bill confessed that he was afraid, too. "That's the spirit of fear attacking you," Fred said. "If you don't deal with it now, it will chase you for the rest of your life."

"What are we supposed to do?" I asked sincerely. At that point in my faith journey, I wasn't that familiar with the reality of the demonic and spiritual realms.

I will never forget the picture he painted for us that night. He started, "If a mangy, rabid dog came into my house and went after my children, what would I do? Would I gently shoo him, hoping he would go away? No! I would chase him out of my house, beating and kicking him—whatever it took! That's what you do with the spirit of fear. Use the Word of God as your weapon and call on the Spirit of God until you chase that spirit out of your house."

Bill and I stayed up for hours praying, rebuking the spirit of fear, singing, reading the Bible, and doing anything that would help us see the power of God overcome our fear. More out of weariness than victory, we finally fell asleep a few hours before we were supposed to leave.

Witch Doctors and the Word

Not only was Fred sending us to a difficult area, but he was staying behind and sending Bill and me with a few local men he had discipled and trained. Before departing, our group prayed together that God would lead us. As the Land Cruiser drove through coffee fields, we passed groups of people along the road and slowed to look at them. Fred's partners in ministry would nod yes or shake their heads no to indicate whether we should stop. Later I realized they had seen visions of certain people in their prayers that morning. As we paused to look at the crowds, they were seeing if these were the ones God had revealed to them during prayer.

"Jimmy, you'll be preaching to the group at our first stop." Those words were a directive, not a request, from our leaders.

The same went for the words I heard from God: *I want you to preach about the realities of heaven and hell.*

That fear I had prayed against quickly reared its head again. I knew there were witch doctors in the crowd, and I wasn't interested in upsetting them. But I remembered Fred's charge to preach the Word boldly, no matter the consequences.

As I spoke confidently about God's power over the devil and the battle between heaven and hell, I heard a demonic voice coming from a man behind me in the bushes. My body froze, and the hairs on the back of my neck stood on end. I prayed for courage and continued preaching. Eventually the growling voice subsided. Despite my fear, and because of the powerful draw of the Holy Spirit, many people came to Jesus that day.

Keeping a Promise

The next day we were supposed to travel to a village Fred had never been to before, but Bill was very sick. As I was explaining the reason we couldn't go on the trip, Fred looked me straight in the eyes and said, "I promised them we will be there, and I never break my promise." That meant I was going, so I gathered my things and got ready to leave.

That particular village was home to a group of believers led by a man Fred had discipled. When the man met Christ, he was passionate. He believed he was being called to pastor and preach, but he had a major problem—he couldn't read. Fred had laid hands on the man and prayed, "God, let him read Your Holy Word!" Miraculously, the man began to read, but he could only read the Bible, nothing else. After that encounter with the power of God, he returned to his village and led most of his community to the Lord.

On the way to that village, we drove through the countryside as far as the Land Cruiser would take us, and then we hiked up the side of a mountain. When we arrived, the love of God overwhelmed us. People ran toward us and embraced us as though we had known each other for a lifetime. I didn't know their language, but somehow the language of God communicated for us. We ate a meal together, a traditional feast called a *mumu*.

After a time of fellowship, the group asked me to preach. At that point in my life, I knew only a couple of Scripture passages by memory, one of which I had learned two nights before: "For God has not given us a spirit of fear, but of power and of love and of a sound mind" (2 Timothy 1:7, NKJV). Since it was fresh on my mind, I thought it would be a good place to start preaching.

We sang a few songs in their common language and then, through two translators, I preached. As I spoke I began to cry. Then those gathered began to cry. The presence of God filled the meeting place. People fell to their knees in prayer. Some raised their hands in thanksgiving, and others lay prostrate on the floor. Heaven had come to earth. When I opened my eyes and looked around, it seemed as though the walls were shaking. I was reminded of Acts 4:31, which reports, "And when they had prayed, the place where they had gathered together was shaken, and they were all filled with the Holy Spirit and began to speak the word of God with boldness."

The book of Acts came alive that day. While people back home were having heady debates about expressions of worship and spiritual gifts, I was experiencing reality—the reality of Jesus among a humble people. This community wasn't putting on a show. They had simply met a Savior and were living out the reality of God's Kingdom by loving Him with all their hearts. That vivid image still sticks in my mind as I yearn for the same thing to happen in communities in our own nation and around the world. This is what church should be.

After Papua New Guinea, I was forever ruined for the ordinary.

> BY GOING TO PLACES WHERE PEOPLE HAVE NEVER HEARD ABOUT JESUS, WE SEE THE POWER OF THE GOSPEL FIRSTHAND. ONCE THE BOOK OF ACTS COMES ALIVE, WE CAN NEVER BE THE SAME. THE POWER OF GOD IS REAL AND ALIVE TODAY.

CHAPTER 4

CULTURE SHOCK AND COMMITMENT

"For I know the plans that I have for you," declares the LORD,
"plans for welfare and not for calamity to give you a future and a hope."

JEREMIAH 29:11

My world was spinning when I returned to Waco from Papua New Guinea. Not only had I lived in an isolated, foreign culture for a summer, but I had also seen God move in mind-blowing, miraculous ways. I had become sensitized to the Holy Spirit and had caught a grand new vision for His Kingdom. I had a new lens, and it was impossible to look at life the way I had before leaving for Papua New Guinea. Coming home, I experienced a serious case of reverse culture shock. Life in Texas had gone on ordinarily while I had experienced the extraordinary, and I wasn't sure how to relate to my own Bible Belt culture.

Confusion to Clarity

To add to my world-spinning confusion, I came back to a crisis at church. The pastor at my church in Waco resigned after confessing his involvement in sexual sin. It caused heartbreak and crisis for hundreds of others, too, including a group of guys I was living with in what we called a "discipleship house." Some in the house wound up pulling away from God because they didn't understand how a pastor who had taught and moved in spiritual gifts could fall in this way. That question led them to doubt the truth of those gifts in the first place.

The combination of culture shock and this church crisis also caused me to question what was real and what wasn't. My experience in Papua New Guinea taught me the vital importance of sharing the gospel, but as I was driving home one day, I found myself screaming, "Lord, You save them! I don't know how to share the gospel. I am not even sure about my own faith." I pulled into the driveway, parked, got out of my car, and started pacing up and down.

"God, what am I supposed to do?" I begged.

I heard a question in response: *Jimmy, is there someone you know who really loves Me?* I immediately thought of my friend Chris.

What is it about Chris that shows you he loves Me? As I thought about it, what stood out was the way Chris loved Jesus with all his heart, soul, mind, and strength.

God asked another question. *Jimmy, can you try to do that?*

I answered timidly, "Yes, Lord, I think I can."

Okay, now what else do you notice about Chris? Chris not only loves Jesus with all his heart, but he also loves and cares for everyone around him.

The Spirit spoke once again with a final question. *What about you—can you love the people in front of you?*

"Yes, Lord, I think I can do that, too," I replied.

God reminded me of a truth found in Scripture: the whole law is wrapped up in a simple statement. I am to love God with all my heart, soul, mind, and strength, and love my neighbor as myself. As long as I can do that, I will always be free.

You don't have to worry about all the unanswered questions. Simply live a life of love, God reassured me.

This truth has anchored me throughout the years. Any time I have questioned different theological or doctrinal perspectives along my own journey, I always come back to the simplicity of loving God and loving people. We are right in the center of God's will when we do these two things.

Spiritual Fathers

Robert Ewing was one of my spiritual fathers. He and his family had been part of the charismatic renewal in Waco in the late 1940s, and Robert had developed a deep love for the church. Robert opened his life to me, becoming a teacher and mentor during my senior year of college. I loved going to his house for lunch and hearing his stories of dramatic miracles and smuggling Bibles into closed countries. His work inspired me to believe God for the impossible. He would talk for hours about the church, convinced it was God's instrument to change the world.

As Robert talked about different Scripture passages that speak about God's design and desire to see the church be all it is called to be, my heart was set on fire. That was the dream I was willing to live and die for—that God would be glorified on earth through His church. If we could learn to be the church and reproduce the church around the world, then the glory of God could be seen in every tribe, tongue, people, and nation. Those days shaped who I am today and created my intense love for God's people, the church.

It was also a season of great brokenness. I knew where I was ultimately going, but I didn't know how to get there. During that time, I spent many hours in a quiet room at Robert's house praying, reading Scripture, and asking God for direction. During those days I had an experience I call "meeting God's authority." It's that place where you come to the realization that He is God and we are not. You come to know that He is big and we are small, and without Him we can do nothing. As I read through the New Testament, rather than becoming encouraged, I became more aware of my own sinfulness. I came to the reality that there is absolutely nothing good in me apart from the grace of God.

One day in particular I was reading 1 Timothy 1:15, where the Apostle Paul declared himself to be the chief of all sinners. As I read it, I found myself saying out loud, "No! *I* am the chief of all sinners." In my turmoil over my own brokenness, I actually grabbed myself by the shirt, threw myself on the floor, and said in tears, "God, there is nothing good in me, but if you will pick me up off this floor and send me where you will, I will be wholly and completely Yours."

Although I have had to recommit daily since that time, it was a defining moment in my life. No longer would life be about me and what I wanted. Instead, I would seek God's heart, and He would be at the center of my decision-making.

No Matter What

Laura, if we choose to get married, there are a few things we have to agree on.

Those words weren't exactly dripping with romance, but they became the foundation of our relationship. Laura and I had been dating for almost a year when I returned from Papua New Guinea. I was asking God whether she should be my wife, but at the same time I recognized that my change of worldview had rattled our relationship. I had come home wanting to live in jungles instead of going down the more conventional path to which we were both accustomed. I needed to know if we were headed down the same path.

After years of working with young people who are in relationships, I have learned that well-meaning believers often get married without a clear sense of focus. Being called to walk the narrow way can easily be cast aside when it comes to love and romance. I knew in my own journey, despite my weaknesses and bumbling, I had to know I could do whatever God was asking on any given day. The woman I married would have to want the same thing, and we would have to be committed together to honoring Him every step of the way.

Laura and I were still dating through my senior year at Baylor and getting more serious all the time. As we began to talk more deliberately about marriage, I knew we would have to discuss how we would live our lives together. I was scared of the idea of losing her, but I knew if we couldn't agree on God's leadership, then we couldn't be married. So I took a deep breath and put it all out there.

"Laura," I began, "if we choose to get married, there are a few things we have to agree on. No matter what, we will listen to and obey God every day of our lives. Whether I like it or you like it, whether my parents or your parents like it, whether our friends like it, it doesn't matter. I have to know that together we can listen to and obey Him no matter what—and that we will go wherever He says and do whatever He wants."

Without hesitation, Laura looked me in the eyes and answered decisively, "That's what I want, too, Jimmy. Nothing else."

Within a couple of months, I asked Laura Mielke to marry me. And she said yes!

Following His Lead

Our first chance to say yes to God came before we were even married. Wanting to build on what I had experienced in Papua New Guinea, my plan was to go to Fuller Theological Seminary so Laura and I could go into ministry together. But as I was walking to the mailbox one morning to send off my application, the Lord interrupted me so strongly that I doubled over in the driveway. He made it perfectly clear that I was not supposed to go to seminary at that time. I walked back to the house and threw the application in the trash, but I didn't have a Plan B. I kept asking God what He had for me instead, but I heard nothing.

Days later, I got an answer I wasn't expecting. As I sat down to study for a finance test, I heard God tell me, "I want you to go into business."

"What? But I gave all that up!" I protested. "When you said, 'Follow Me,' I gave up my pursuit of business and chose to follow You instead."

His response was definitive: "Trust Me, and I will lead you the right way."

Laura and I had already committed to say yes no matter what, so I began looking for business opportunities. One opened up in Houston for a medical supply company, so after graduation I packed up and moved. Laura stayed in Waco to finish school.

I decided that if God had called me to business, then I would go for it with the same passion I would have dedicated to seminary. Still, I knew the business world would be challenging, so every morning I read and meditated on the words in John 15:1-15, praying I could adapt them to my life. *I am the vine, you are the branches; he who abides in Me and I in him, he bears much fruit, for apart from Me you can do nothing.* The phrase that played on a loop in my mind was apart from Me you can do nothing. That summer I became so addicted to Jesus—to abiding in Him—that I found it was too difficult to live apart from

Him. I truly didn't want to do anything without Him.

Out of that simple, abiding relationship, I saw God move powerfully while I worked in business. Vocationally, I was able to sell products and serve customers with excellence. I was also able to share Christ, see people healed, and see lives redirected. God was so near that at times I could tangibly feel His presence. Some of my fondest memories of walking intimately with the Lord are from those days. No one had talked to me about how to be a Christian businessman, but it happened because I sought to follow Jesus. I learned that wherever God puts me, the answer to bearing fruit in that place is to listen to and obey God.

After months of working in Houston, my general manager, also a believer, asked me what God had for my life. I poured out my heart to him, sharing the depths of my burden for God's work around the world. He suggested I take a few days off to go to Waco and pray with Laura about God's direction for our future. So I hopped in the car and headed north to Waco.

On my way, the Lord spoke both revelation and direction to me. When I first went to Baylor, I was seeking a reputation, but this time He would bring me back to lose my reputation. Second, He wanted to teach me to love Laura as Christ loved the church. I got into town on a Wednesday evening and went straight to the service at Highland Baptist Church. There, God spoke to me again, perhaps more clearly than I had heard up to that point: *I want you to stay and watch Me build My church from the bottom up.*

I had absolutely no idea what that meant, but I knew God had spoken. I quit my job and moved back to Waco.

Make Your Bed

After moving back, I continued to spend time praying and seeking God's direction at Robert Ewing's house. One day he shared that his church needed host homes for some visiting missionaries who were attending a conference. I opened up my apartment, and God brought a man into my life named Ron Higgins. God had used Ron mightily in India and Pakistan, preaching at massive crusades where thousands of people were saved and healed. More than anything, though, Ron was a humble and tender man of God.

When Ron stayed with my roommates and me, I asked if I could spend time with him. He said, "Sure, why don't you meet me first thing tomorrow—at five o'clock."

I nodded yes, but all I could think was, *You mean five in the morning? What, are we going fishing?*

When we met, Ron told me that the first hour of the day was for prayer. *Awesome*, I thought. *What a great idea.* Ron went to his corner, and I went to mine and began to pray. An hour later Ron woke me up and told me it was time to study the Word.

Wonderful, I thought. *I love the Bible!* I began reading and soon started meditating as well. Meditation, as you may know, sometimes happens with eyes closed. And as you might have guessed, Ron had to wake me again, this time while I was drooling on the open pages of my Bible.

I followed Ron for four days, driving him around and sticking as close to his side as time allowed. Everyone he met soon discovered that he knew Jesus. He would pray for people, show them love, or encourage them in some way. Often he boldly shared the gospel on the spot. I was inspired to witness such a lifestyle of love, both for God and others.

When we had time, I would ask Ron to tell his stories of seeing God's power at work in India and Pakistan. Instead, he consistently turned toward me and asked to hear my stories. On the fifth morning we spent together, we talked at the breakfast table. We spoke of nations coming to faith and God revealing Himself mightily in power. The presence of God was so strong we could feel it. It seemed as if Jesus Himself was sitting at the table with us. Then Ron put his hand on my shoulder and declared, "I have a word for you."

He began proclaiming an incredible prophecy over my life. It was intense. God was in our midst, and His presence was undeniable. Overwhelmed by the amazing words Ron spoke, I thought, *Finally, the hour of God's anointed power on my life has come! I've read about things like this, and now it's happening to me.* By the time Ron finished, visions of worldwide revival danced in my head, and

I saw myself standing on stage leading a hundred thousand people to Christ. As we wiped our eyes and gained our composure, I turned to Ron and asked eagerly, "So what now? Where do I go from here?"

"Jimmy," he answered, "I've been living across the hall from you for about a week now, and your room is a mess."

That wasn't even close to what I was expecting to hear. *Gee, I hope it didn't bother you*, I thought. Then I asked again, "Okay, but what are we going to do about the worldwide revival, Ron?"

"I don't think you understand," he went on to explain. "Unless you first learn to make your bed, you will never be able to administrate great things of God. Remember, Jesus said in Luke 16:10, 'He who is faithful in a very little thing is faithful also in much.'"

Within seconds, I was tumbling from a prophetic mountaintop into a sobering valley of reality.

"How's your prayer life?" Ron continued. I told him I was into praying an hour a day.

He probed some more. "How often do you do that, Jimmy?"

God's presence hung heavily in the room. I remembered stories from Scripture about what happened to people who lied in the presence of God, so I opted for honesty. I looked down. "Only a couple times a week," I admitted.

Ron challenged me to be faithful in prayer. He suggested I start with five or ten minutes a day until I could become consistent seven days a week, 365 days a year. Then I could go to fifteen minutes, and so on. "Make prayer your first priority in the morning as an act of your will to depend on God alone throughout the day," he encouraged.

"What about your Bible reading? Have you read the whole Bible?"

I thought about it. Surely I had. I loved to read the Bible. Wouldn't I eventually get to a point where I'd read it all?

Ron challenged me again. "The Bible is the anchor for our souls. It transforms our minds and hearts and lays the foundation for our entire belief system. We must be constantly in the Word," he said.

"What about evangelism, Jimmy?"

I thought I had a great answer for that one because of my amazing summer sharing the gospel in jungles. But Ron wasn't interested in those stories. He wanted to know if everyone in my life knew that I knew Jesus. He asked bluntly, "Are you ashamed of Christ?"

Systematically Ron went through areas of my life, asking hard questions. Moment by moment I shrunk in humility. Before the end of that conversation, we were on the floor, crying out to God and asking Him to make me a faithful man.

It all seemed to make sense in that one experience with Ron: God had wonderful plans for my life, but they would never fully come to pass unless I could learn to be obedient and faithful. Jeremiah 29:11–13 puts it this way: "'For I know the plans that I have for you,' declares the LORD, 'plans for welfare and not for calamity to give you a future and a hope. Then you will call upon Me and come and pray to Me, and I will listen to you. You will seek Me and find Me when you search for Me with all your heart.'"

So I began a journey of spiritual discipline. I prayed first thing every day, sought God in His Word, fasted regularly, shared the good news of Jesus with everyone and anyone, discipled others, and created a lifestyle of servanthood in the context of community. I am thankful God was gracious enough to bring Ron Higgins into my life right when I needed it. Not only did God reveal part of His dream to me through Ron, but He also taught me how to live a life through which those dreams could come to pass. Without that lesson, I would not have seen God's dreams fulfilled in my life.

Called to Ministry

I have never thought of myself as a pastor. I know that sounds strange since I've been a pastor for many years. What I mean is, I've never thought of my position as a vocational move, calling, or career. I never set out to be a pastor. I just kept answering one question: Am I doing what Jesus is saying? All I know is if the answer is yes, then I'm doing what I'm supposed to be doing.

When I returned from Papua New Guinea, I thought I'd found what I was supposed to do with the rest of my life—go across the world to share God's message with people who've never heard it. Then God told me to go into business, so I thought I would live for Jesus in the business world. In my heart, though, I knew what I wanted more than anything else was to share God's message.

I went to the church elders for counsel. I told them there was nothing I wanted to do more than serve God's people full-time, but I wasn't sure whether I was called. Charles Davis, the senior pastor, led the way in giving me counsel.

"I have four boys," he began. "What if one of my sons came to me and said, 'Dad, more than anything in the world I want to lead God's people, but I'm not sure if I'm called'? Unless I knew there was something else he should be doing, what I would want more than anything is to support him."

"Jimmy," he continued, "God has obviously gotten hold of your heart for the nations and for His people. As elders, we do not sense that God has called you to anything other than that. You can be confident that your Father in heaven has put that on your heart, and He will back you up for your future."

I walked out convinced that my Father in heaven had called Laura and me to serve His people, no matter the cost, whether it was vocational or otherwise. I knew this was where I needed to spend my energy and my life. God was forming His destiny and purpose in my life.

Psalm 103:7 says, "He made known His ways to Moses, His acts to the sons of Israel." It is always God's desire to show us His ways, not just His acts. I was excited about what He had done in Papua New Guinea, but God made sure I also knew His ways: through simple humility I can stay close to Him in order to see His power and purposes fulfilled.

You can, too.

BROKENNESS IS GOD'S PREPARATION FOR OUR ABILITY TO BE USED BY HIM. WHEN WE SUBMIT TO THE WORK OF GOD IN US, THERE IS NO LIMIT TO WHAT HE CAN DO THROUGH US.

CHAPTER 5

JUST DO WHAT'S NEXT

But we have this treasure in earthen vessels, so that the surpassing greatness of the power will be of God and not from ourselves.

2 CORINTHIANS 4:7

Laura and I married on December 20, 1986. Even before we started our life together, we had overseas missions in mind. We were both burdened by God's heart for the nations and were convinced that God was going to send us out. We began looking for opportunities to serve overseas with Youth With A Mission (YWAM), but God began leading us in a different direction.

Here's what I've learned since then: God calls us to obey and respond to the next step before us; and when we do, He will shape, lead, and guide our lives. Our job is to trust Him, believe Him, and say yes to the next thing He is telling us to do. When we do that, we will be able to look back and see His glory displayed in our lives.

Bigger Dreams

Two weeks before our wedding, Laura and I went to a conference in Dallas with some of the leadership from Highland Baptist Church. The speaker called for young leaders to come forward to receive prayer. Since I was not a leader, I stayed back, but Mark Buckner, the college pastor at Highland, walked to the front.

As I watched Mark receive prayer, I heard God saying to me, "I am calling you to serve this man. He has carried My dreams in his heart, and I want you to support him. Ask him to forgive you for the ways you have judged him over the years and tell him you are here to serve."

I went forward, confessed my sins, and told Mark I was going to serve him. Over the next couple of days, Laura and I fasted and prayed for clarification about how we were to serve Mark. During another meeting two days later, a leader from Romania prayed over us, saying, "God has been preparing you. Within the next few months, you will begin training young men and women to be sent to the four corners of the earth."

Well, that's neat, I thought, *but he must have it wrong.* In the first place, I had just come through the most broken time in my life. I wasn't prepared to train others—I was falling apart. Besides, no one was asking us to train anyone.

It turned out I was the one who had it wrong.

Shortly after Laura and I got married, we got together with Mark and his wife, Susan. We talked at length about what we thought the church could be if it had both a local and global vision. We all desired to see young men and women from the college group trained and sent out to the nations. The four of us talked and prayed, and together we came up with a proposal to submit to the Highland Baptist Church elders. It went like this:

> *God is challenging us, the local church, to own the process of developing, training, and sending people to the nations. Typically those who want to be trained for full-time vocational ministry either go to seminary or serve through a parachurch organization. God has used and continues to use those avenues powerfully today, but we want to send out teams from the local church who have learned to live the Kingdom values of loving Jesus, discipleship, and evangelism in the context*

of community. Out of their experiences together, they could repro-
duce local churches anywhere in the world.

Our simple dream started with a discipleship training school. We would challenge students to commit to one year: nine months of intense discipleship in the city, followed by three months of serving overseas.

As we were preparing, we heard about a program at Phoenix First Assembly of God called Master's Commission, so we visited and discovered it was similar to what God was putting on our hearts. After combining elements of that program, elements of YWAM's Discipleship Training School, and several of our own ideas, we started our discipleship school in the fall of 1987.

The Next Thing

As we worked to get the discipleship school ready, Laura and I were working part-time jobs to make ends meet. One of my brilliant ideas was to start a lawn-mowing business. It turned out not to be such a great idea. Not long into the venture, I found myself spending almost every dollar I made on repairs and equipment maintenance. At that rate, we would have had nothing when the school began. As I was driving down the freeway one day on the way to mow another lawn, I grew increasingly anxious. I asked, "God, am I just crazy, or is this really You leading us?"

God spoke to me as clearly as I have ever heard Him: *If you will simply obey the next thing I'm telling you to do, you will be able to be a part of the greatest revival the world has ever seen.*

I pulled to the side of the road and cried. It hit me that this dream wasn't just something we had come up with, but it was truly from God. Although I didn't know much, I knew I could do the next thing He was telling me to do. Over the years, that has become our mode of leadership: we ask the Lord for the next step, and even if we can't see the big picture, we can choose to say yes today. Out of our simple obedience, God has been weaving a tapestry of His grace.

As I waited on the Lord about everything that was before us, He gave me two key Scriptures. The first was Isaiah 58:11–12:

"And the LORD will continually guide you,

And satisfy your desire in scorched places,

And give strength to your bones;

And you will be like a watered garden,

And like a spring of water whose waters do not fail.

Those from among you will rebuild the ancient ruins;

You will raise up the age-old foundations;

And you will be called the repairer of the breach,

The restorer of the streets in which to dwell."

While I wasn't sure what all of it meant, I began to use that verse as a guide for everything we did. The second Scripture God gave me was Isaiah 43:18–19:

"Do not call to mind the former things,

Or ponder things of the past.

Behold, I will do something new,

Now it will spring forth;

Will you not be aware of it?

I will even make a roadway in the wilderness,

Rivers in the desert."

Early on, God gave us faith to believe Him for new things, to believe He would make a way where there was no way. Again and again, I have seen these Scriptures become reality in our lives. God speaks prophetically through His Word and then fulfills it through those who trust Him and faithfully wait on His promises.

Discipleship School Starts

We kicked off our discipleship school that fall with eight students. Each morning we memorized Scripture, studied the Bible, prayed together, and received teaching. In the afternoons students started different outreaches in our community and served through various ministries of the church.

The school's curriculum grew out of what Ron Higgins had taught me: the simple practices of prayer and fasting, reading the Word, evangelism, making disciples, and serving others. We believed if students learned to walk in relationship with Jesus and actually live the disciplines—instead of just talking about them—then the transformation they experienced would catapult them outward to change the world in God's power.

During that first year, God did incredible things in our hearts and through our lives. Some of my fondest memories relate to evangelism. In learning to be bold with our faith, we would preach the gospel in university commons areas, in the middle of restaurants, and everywhere in between. Some may have called us foolish—in fact, I'm sure of it—but we didn't want to let anyone miss the opportunity to hear the good news of Jesus.

The critical piece of evangelism was learning to listen to the Holy Spirit throughout the day. I remember walking through our neighborhood, asking the Lord to show me who I should talk to. There were several people in their yards, so the question was, "Which one?" I felt the Spirit strongly direct me to a woman down the street, and as I walked toward her I asked the Lord what to say. When I reached her I engaged her in conversation and found out her name was Sarah.

I asked Sarah, "Do you know Jesus?"

"No," she replied, "but I just got out of the hospital, and while I was there, I had a dream of falling into a black hole. I could tell I was falling away from a beautiful light, and I was screaming out to that light. Can you tell me what that light was?"

I was blown away. I gladly explained that the light was Jesus, and I believed He had spared her life so she could hear the gospel and be saved. Sarah gave her heart to the Lord that day. Her husband, Michael, eventually gave his life to the Lord as well, and Laura and I were able to spend time discipling them as a couple.

Living by Faith

When the elders of Highland gave us permission to start the training school, they told us that no finances were available to pay a staff or fund the needed resources. If we were going to do this thing, it would have to be done—and funded—by faith and volunteerism.

Laura and I had been reading about George Müller, a pastor in England in the nineteenth century who trusted God completely for finances. He took care of thousands of orphans, never asking anyone for financial assistance, but praying daily for God's provision. His journals of seeing God provide gave us faith to believe that God could do the same for us.

We were both excited and sobered by the opportunity to walk by faith as Mr. Müller did. Going into the discipleship school year, we did everything we could to cut our expenses. We moved into a lower-income neighborhood, sold many of our personal belongings, and waited with faith to see God move. It was a challenging and exciting adventure for us.

In the fall Laura started working as the secretary for our youth pastor while I worked with the training school. It didn't take long for us to realize it was better for us to minister together, but we didn't know how to make that work financially. By faith, Laura quit her job in December even though we didn't know how it would play out. The demand for mowing lawns had dried up, and we definitely needed to see God move financially on our behalf.

Over the next several months, we saw God provide in ways that would set us on a life-shaping course of trust. One night we invited a man over for dinner. We had no food in the cabinets, and we wondered if we should have him over at all. The man was a friend of Robert Ewing's, though, so I told Laura, "Look, he knows Jesus, so let's just pray and trust God. He'll understand if there isn't anything to eat."

As he pulled into the driveway, I greeted him in the front yard. He stepped out of the car and said, "Hey, I just had to put my mother in a nursing facility, but I had bought groceries for her house. I was praying about what to do with them, and God told me to bring them to you. Would you mind receiving these?"

Would I mind? "Brother, you don't understand," I answered. "You just provided your own dinner."

God provided many miracles in the area of food. We invited Sarah and

Michael, the couple who had come to know Jesus, and their two children over for dinner. Again, we didn't have enough to feed them all—only a few noodles and a little spaghetti sauce. They were new believers, so we prayed about what to do.

I said to Laura, "Honey, God has multiplied food before. Let's take what we have, cook it as if it were a feast, and trust God." That night six people ate all they wanted, with some left over. Just like the crowd of five thousand gathered on a Galilean hillside, we saw food multiply before our eyes.

In the course of the evening, Sarah quietly told Laura that she didn't want to go to church because she didn't have a nice dress to wear. Laura reassured her that what she wore didn't matter, but Sarah was still insecure about coming.

Laura asked her, "If you could have any dress, what color would you want?" Sarah answered she would love to have a yellow dress, size ten.

We were on a seriously tight budget those days, but we really wanted to buy a dress for Sarah. Later, Laura asked me, "What would Jesus do in this situation?"

We thought about going to Wal-Mart to buy the dress, but we decided Jesus would go all out and get the best. So we went to a department store at the mall. As we went in to look around, Laura saw a sale rack. Sure enough, there was a size ten yellow dress, seventy-five percent off. For just ten dollars we were able to buy a new, beautiful dress for Sarah. She wore it every week when she came to church.

During that season we never missed a bill payment, although sometimes we cut it to the very last minute. Once, we owed $53.24 with no way to pay it. The next day when it was due, we got a refund check in the mail from the gas utility company for $53.24. It was what we needed to the penny, and we praised God for His provision.

During that Christmas season, God led us in creative ways to give gifts to friends and family and in sharing with each other. For our second Christmas together, Laura and I bought a double cassette of Keith Green's greatest hits. I wrapped one and gave it to her, and she wrapped the other and gave it to me. The next year we bought his gold twin cassette set and did the same thing. These were the best of times as our hearts were free, and we enjoyed the simple things in life.

Times were lean, but we always had enough. Paul wrote in Philippians 4:11–12, "I have learned to be content in whatever circumstances I am. I know how to get along with humble means, and I also know how to live in prosperity; in any and every circumstance I have learned the secret of being filled and going hungry, both of having abundance and suffering need." God was teaching us contentment. I like to say He was refining our "suburban souls" so we might be free to live with Him in any way—or place—He chooses.

The Gift of Giving

That season was about learning to receive God's provision, but it was also about learning how to give out of our need. Sometimes the Lord led us to give away money we needed for bills, gas, or food. Once a group of missionaries from YWAM came to do a presentation at our church. At that time we had enough food, so we volunteered to be a host home to provide a missionary with a place to stay, a breakfast, and a sack lunch.

After the presentation we were at our home, sitting around the table talking. This young missionary told us he was believing God for the four thousand dollars he needed to work with street kids in Brazil. Laura and I had a bill for one hundred dollars due the next day, and we had only twenty dollars to our name. As he excused himself for a few moments, I turned to Laura and said, "We only have twenty dollars to give. What do you think?"

She said, "I think we ought to give all that we have. We've trusted God this far, so let's trust Him with everything." We gladly gave the young missionary twenty dollars, apologizing that we didn't have more to give, but assuring him we would pray that God would multiply it for his needs.

The next morning, after we sent him on his way, we went into his room to pick up towels and sheets and found a thank-you note. It read something like this: *Thank you so much for having me in your home. It was a delight to be with you and talk about the Kingdom of God. As I was praying this morning, God showed me that your need is greater than mine and that I was to give you this one hundred dollars. I pray that it is God's provision for whatever you need.*

How exciting it was to see God provide through both receiving and giving. During those first two years of leading the training school, our annual income never exceeded nine thousand dollars, but we were able to give half of that away. God sovereignly worked to take care of us. It was lessons of giving, not just receiving, that set patterns for the rest of our lives. I've found that if we won't give out of the little we do have, then we won't give out of abundance either. "Give," the Bible says, "and it will be given to you" (Luke 6:38). God takes care of those who have open hands and open hearts.

Sticking It Out

The spring of 1988 brought a whole new set of challenges for our discipleship school. A fire completely gutted the building at Highland where we had been meeting, and within the next few months, the senior pastor, one of the associate pastors, and the worship leader all resigned. These men had supported our journey, even when many others were skeptical and critical. In a short period of time, the school had lost its home and support.

After the fire, the school started meeting at our house. Without the support we'd had the first semester and with the physical limitations and hardships we faced, I began to wonder if it was even worth planning a second year. Maybe it was time for Laura and me to move on from Highland. Perhaps God was trying to redirect us.

About the time I was struggling with these questions, I met a man from YWAM named Dean Sherman, who was speaking at Highland. I met with him privately and shared my concerns. Secretly I wanted Dean to sympathize and counsel me to move on. To my surprise, though, he had very different words for me.

"Jimmy, whose vision is this anyway?" he asked. "Do you expect everyone to jump up and down and get excited just because you have a vision from God? If you're not willing to put three to five years into it, your vision will never be fulfilled. So either quit now or stop whining. If it's God's vision, He will make a way."

Those were tough words, but they were exactly what we needed to hear. At the time only two women had signed up for the fall session of the second year, but

Laura and I committed that even if there were only two students, we would obey the next thing God had for us. We would still do the school in faith. By the time we started our second year, seven eager, passionate students were ready to go.

Shortly after, God gave me a word for the future of the discipleship school and the expanding work He would have us do. He told me that the first five years would lay a foundation, years six through ten would be a season of growth, and years eleven through fifteen would be a time of maturing.

Our discipleship school has been going for twenty-six years now. Looking back, I see how God's Word came true over the first fifteen years and laid the foundation for where we are today.

By the end of the 2012–2013 school year, more than 2,700 students had graduated from the Antioch Training Schools through Waco and our churches around the world. When Mark and Susan Buckner and Laura and I first talked about starting a discipleship training school, we could not have imagined all that God had planned. From humble beginnings to experiencing the awesome power and provision of God, the Antioch Training Schools have been an example of what it looks like for God to birth His dreams through a willing people.

GOD IS COMMITTED TO MOVING THROUGH HIS PEOPLE TO CHANGE THE WORLD. OUR OBEDIENCE TO HIS WORD AND HIS VOICE PUTS US RIGHT IN THE MIDDLE OF HIS PURPOSE AND PLANS FOR OUR LIVES.

CHAPTER 6

MIRACLES IN THE NATIONS

But prove yourselves doers of the word,
and not merely hearers who delude themselves.

JAMES 1:22

After nine months of classroom training and serving the church and community in Waco, the first training school class was ready for its three-month overseas summer outreach. Before we left for Iceland, England, and the Netherlands, we made a decision together to trust God for our finances and to mention our needs to no one. It was no longer just Laura and me. Now, our team of eight decided to believe together that God would provide. Sufficient funds came in so we could leave, but there was enough need left to require a few more miracles along the way.

In Reykjavik, Iceland, the eight of us stayed in a small two-bedroom apartment. Three single girls were in one bedroom, three single guys were in the living room, and Laura and I were in the corner room. We had plenty of opportunities to worship, pray, and learn from one another in those tight quarters.

Pizza Provision in Reykjavik

The church we were working with had generously agreed to provide the apartment and stock our refrigerator if we would just come. One Saturday night, after being there for two weeks of our one-month outreach, we ran out of food. They had provided wonderfully but had not checked on us for a few days. As we got up that Sunday morning, everyone was asking what we were going to do. I said, "One thing we are not going to do is mention our needs. We've come this far, so let's watch God provide."

So, with tentative excitement, we went to church hoping someone would invite us to lunch. After we had ministered in the church service and had a great time with the people there, we returned to our apartment with no lunch. While we were all tempted to grumble and complain, I had an idea. "Okay," I offered, "let's figure out specifically what to ask God for. If we had lunch, what would we want?"

The final consensus was pizza—the kind that was cut in squares—with salad and Coke to go along with it. "If that's what we want," I said, "then let's ask God for it and have a time of worship." With a little bit of grumbling, we began to do just that. We hadn't prayed for more than five minutes when the phone rang. It was the wife of one of the elders from the church we were working with.

"A couple of families are meeting at our house for lunch," she told me. "We've got a lot of extra food, and we'd love to have you join us. Would you like to come over?"

I hung up the phone and shouted, "Guys, it's time to eat lunch!"

When we got to the house and prayed together for the lunch, the hostess said, "I hope this food is okay. I made pizza, and we have salad and Coca Cola." Not only was it pizza, but it was also cut in squares just as we had asked. We laughed, shouted, and rejoiced as we shared with them the story of God's wonderful—and very specific—provision. I knew the miracle of the loaves and fish, but this was the first time I'd seen the miracle of pizza and Coke.

Our cabinets were full the rest of the time, but more than anything, our hearts were full, knowing that God sees even our basic needs and is willing to provide above and beyond even what we could ask or think.

In Iceland we saw God's practical provision, but more importantly, we experienced the power of God in dynamic ways. One night as we worshipped in someone's home, a neighbor heard us and knocked on the door. We welcomed him in and began to pray for him. As we prayed he began to shake under the awesome presence of God's Spirit falling on him. The man gave his life to Jesus.

A few minutes later there was another knock on the door. A different neighbor entered, and the same thing happened: we prayed, he shook, and then he gave his life to Christ. It reminded me of Acts 2:42-47, which describes how the church met from house to house and lived in a way that people were being added to them day by day. We were experiencing the Scriptures coming to life right before our eyes.

Healing and Hope in England

From Iceland we went to work with a church in Aldershot, England. Ministry there was difficult because many people were closed to the gospel message, but every day we went out to perform dramas, preach on the streets, and share the gospel house to house.

After doing a drama in the town square and then preaching, we encountered an atheist who had broken his leg a week earlier. He mocked us openly, but the students still shared the gospel with him and offered to pray for him. Reluctantly he let them. They simply prayed, "Lord, heal this man and show him that You are real." He politely dismissed himself, saying, "Okay, I have to get to a doctor's appointment." Then he left us. At the doctor's office they took an x-ray, and he learned his leg was completely healed.

That man was the principal of a local school. He went to work and told more than three hundred students that some people had prayed for him in the name of Jesus, and he had been healed. He remembered the name of the church we were working with and called the church office asking to speak to a pastor. After hearing his story, the pastor led him to the Lord on the phone. The following Sunday, he came to church to testify of God's goodness.

On another occasion in Aldershot, as we went door to door, a woman answered when we knocked. We offered to pray with her and share our testimony, but she became irate, saying, "Don't tell me that Jesus loves me or cares! God doesn't care about me!"

"Why do you think that?" I asked.

"Look at my son," she said. A little boy, who looked about six years old, appeared. "He has mental problems and was just diagnosed with colon cancer."

Our hearts broke with her. We told her that we wanted to pray that God would heal her son. Softened by the compassion we showed for her son, she let us lay hands on him and pray. What a delightful little boy he was, smiling and hugging us while we prayed over him.

That was the next-to-last day before we left England. The boy was having surgery the next morning, and we went to visit him in the hospital to see how he was doing. When we arrived the mother had this incredible look of excitement and shock on her face.

"What happened?" we asked.

She said that when the doctors ran one last scan while preparing for the surgery, they found that the cancer was gone. She held up the images and said, "The cancer is gone. God has healed my son."

As we hugged her and cried together, we rejoiced over a God who sees the pain and need in people's hearts and shows up in miraculous ways.

Set Free in Amsterdam

From England, we went to the Netherlands to work with YWAM. They had a base in Amsterdam from which they did outreach all over the city, specifically among prostitutes and drug addicts. Every day we would go out to the streets to share the gospel. In the evenings we would follow up with new believers.

Laura and I first met Keith while walking together in Amsterdam. He was from Connecticut and approached us for money to get out of the country, saying he was addicted to heroin and wanted to be free from his addiction. While I don't usually give money to drug addicts, I felt on that particular occasion I should.

After I gave Keith the four dollars I had, he thanked me and was about to run off when I said, "Keith, you need Jesus!"

He replied, "Oh, whatever. Thanks, man."

"No, Keith, let me pray for you." I put my hand on his shoulder and said, "Lord, reveal Your heart to him. Keith needs You, and You want to show Him You are real."

When I finished praying, Keith screamed, "What was that, man?"

I answered, "That was Jesus, and He is after you."

"Whoa, dude, that's crazy. That's crazy, man," he said as he ran off. I was so burdened for Keith that all day I prayed I would encounter him again. The next day while I was heading through the red-light district to do ministry, I ran into him.

"Hey, man," Keith said, "that deal yesterday was a blow-away. That was amazing. What was that?"

"Man, that was Jesus," I said.

"I thought it was just the power of the mind, you know? Like, you put your hand on somebody's shoulder and activate the power of positive thinking or something."

"No, it's not positive thinking. It's Jesus!" I assured him.

We sat on the street curb in the rain, and Keith told me his story. Like the prodigal son, He had come to Amsterdam to live a lifestyle of parties and pleasure. After getting hooked on heroin, losing all his money, and becoming wanted by the law, he was living on the streets and constantly on the run.

Before he left that day, I offered to pray for him again, but this time I told him I wouldn't use my hands. "Keith, you need to know it's God's presence and power that is on you. It's not about me or anybody else." So I prayed again, "Lord Jesus, show him You are real and pour out Your Spirit on him."

As we sat there on a curb in the red-light district with rain pouring down on us, it was like heaven on earth. God came and touched Keith again with His power and presence.

We agreed to meet that night to talk about drug rehab. As we met near Central Station in downtown Amsterdam, I challenged Keith with his need to receive Christ. He listened to the gospel again and understood that he needed to respond to God. When he decided that he needed and wanted Jesus, I felt I should not tell him how to pray. I said, "Keith, you know your need, and God is willing to listen. I want you to get on your knees here with me and cry out to God with whatever your need is."

As Keith knelt beside me on the street, he offered a desperate prayer of his need for God's forgiveness and power in his life. Once again it seemed as if heaven had come to earth—we were caught in an incredible vortex of God's grace and power. When we opened our eyes after praying, I looked up to see a circle of Japanese tourists clicking photos of us. They must have thought we were part of the crazy scene in Amsterdam!

After that experience Keith agreed to go to a drug rehab center called Victory Outreach, which helps people quit cold turkey. At the center, people sit and pray with addicts through those most difficult first days. After two days, though, Keith ran away.

I scoured the darkest reaches of the city looking for Keith with Lars, a friend I'd met from Sweden. We looked under bridges, in seedy hotels, and in the drug houses of Amsterdam. My heart broke as I saw the devastation of people's lives when they were addicted to heroin and caught up in the sex industry. But we did not find Keith.

A few evenings later when I was speaking at the YWAM base, someone came to me and said there was a man outside looking for me, saying he wanted to kill me. When I asked who the man was, they said, "It's some guy from America named Keith."

"Oh, he won't kill me," I said, and I went outside to meet him.

"Man, you #&*!" he shouted, cursing at and pushing me. "What did you do to me?"

In animated language, he explained that after he had run away from the rehab center, he approached a woman at an ATM to ask for money. When he tried to talk to her, though, his words sounded like gibberish. "My tongue was glued to the roof of my mouth, and I couldn't speak," he said. "What did you do to me? I can't even talk. What's happening to me?"

I was reminded of Psalm 137:6, which says, "May my tongue cling to the roof of my mouth if I do not remember you."

"Keith," I said, "God is after you. He's after your heart."

At that point he broke. "What do I do?" he asked. "I don't know what to do."

I called my friend Lars over and told Keith we would pray with him as long as he needed. We prayed on the streets of Amsterdam until well after 2:00 in the morning. About 1:30 a.m., the breakthrough came. God was powerfully touching Keith. He looked up with tears streaming down his face and grabbed me by the shirt and screamed, "He loves me! He loves me! He loves me!"

I couldn't help but shout back, "He loves me, too! He loves me, too!" In that moment, once again, I realized that God's great love and power has set us all free.

It was a beautiful night of breakthrough for Keith, but when we met again to pray together the next evening, we all felt that something was blocking him from total freedom. As we waited on the Lord, a picture of Keith's father came to my mind. When I mentioned his father and suggested that he needed to forgive, Keith freaked out. He started pulling his hair and pacing around like a caged animal.

"No, no!" he cried. "He's hurt me too bad. I can't do it."

"Keith, God wants to fully deliver you, but you have to forgive," I said.

"I don't know if I can," he cried.

My heart was broken for him as he left that night, not sure where he would go from there. Two days later he came to see me before we left for the States. I embraced him and talked about God's goodness. I appealed to him again to respond to the Lord. Again, he said he wanted to, but it was just too hard.

I prayed for Keith every day for the next four months, not knowing what had happened to him. Then I got a letter, a photo, and a recording of Keith testifying to what the Lord had done in his life. After our team left Amsterdam, Keith took a severe nosedive back into drugs. Then he was in a car accident and had to spend a couple of days in the hospital. During that time he realized he had to get free somehow. Knowing that in jail he could get methadone to help him taper off drugs, he went to the judge who works the area around the red-light district and confessed to several crimes. The judge accused him of wanting to get in jail for food and a place to stay.

"Either you put me in jail, or I will throw a brick through your car window,"

Keith threatened. The judge dismissed him. So Keith walked outside, found a large chunk of cement, and threw it through the window of the judge's BMW. He was immediately arrested and thrown in jail.

During that next month in jail, Keith kicked drugs. A friend from YWAM visited every day to share with him what it means to walk with Jesus. When he got out of jail, he went to a YWAM rehabilitation facility. There, he received intensive discipleship and grew quickly in the Lord. Before long he was back on the streets, but this time he was preaching the gospel instead of shooting up. Keith led many people to the Lord and even started traveling with YWAM leaders to share his testimony with thousands during evangelistic outreaches.

Keith has been through his ups and downs over the years, but God saved him and set him free. Today Keith advocates for people with HIV and AIDS and has been used throughout the Netherlands to comfort others and see lives healed. His journey to freedom is such a testimony of God's patient grace and power to seek out and deliver anyone who will look His way.

Youth Revival in Iceland

The second year of our discipleship school, the summer of 1989, we took a team of nine back to Iceland, where the church in Reykjavik asked us to lead a youth camp. On the last night of camp, we waited on the Lord to show us what we should preach about. While in prayer one of the students saw a picture of a cross. So Brad, a discipleship school graduate who was serving as the Reykjavik church's youth pastor, preached out of Isaiah 53 about the cross.

At the end of the message, a young man came forward for prayer. As we lifted our hands to pray for him, the Spirit of God came on him, and he fell back. Suddenly a spiritual barrier in the room broke, and people began calling out, "I want prayer! I want prayer!"

For the next four hours, the Lord visited us in a mighty way. God's power was on us just as in the book of Acts. People were set free. The sick were healed. Many came to salvation, and we all experienced the awesome power of God in that place.

After about three and a half hours, I broke away from the crowd and went out on the deck of the conference center. I began to praise and thank God for showing up, answering our prayers, and moving in power. For years I'd prayed that I would see the gifts of the Holy Spirit found in the book of Acts come alive, and that night I had seen it with my own eyes. But part of me still felt empty inside. Just seeing the power of God didn't satisfy me.

Then God spoke to me, saying, "Remember, My gifts are sent to help and heal people's lives. The gifts are for them, but I am for you. I will always be enough for you." The gifts of the Holy Spirit are not meant to thrill us or even to prove God is who He says He is. They were sent to help hurting people find what they need. For those of us who get to be the vessels of that power, our need is only satisfied in knowing God fully.

That night, as God moved among us, a group of university students and young professionals, who had been partying in one of the retreat cabins near our gathering, began to watch the scene. In their drunken state they began to mock us. We talked to them and invited them to come to church that next evening. Surprisingly, five showed up.

As we started the service, one of those guys fell to his knees crying and asking God for help. As we prayed for him, he exclaimed that he needed to be free. I told him he needed to pour out all of the alcohol and drugs he had in his pockets. He went with me to the bathroom and poured out everything he had and flushed it down the toilet. That night all five of those guys came to Christ.

We continued to see remarkable things among the youth in Reykjavik. We were in a revival. The youth would bring their friends to our meetings, and God would show up. People were saved and set free all around us.

Perhaps the most powerful thing I learned during that revival was that prior to our arrival, the mothers in the church had been fervently praying for the youth in that area. Their intercession had tilled the hard ground so the gospel could be planted. As a team, we simply had the privilege of harvesting the fruit of their prayers.

The Horseshoe Bar

From Iceland the team went to the city of Banff in northern Scotland. There we met Joe Ewen, a fisherman who had become a fisher of men—a pastor with a passion for church planting. Joe had planted Riverside Church in Banff and was in the process of planting a couple of other churches in the area as well. Joe had a heart and vision for Banff and for communities around the world. When we met Joe that first day, God once again answered my prayer for spiritual fathers. He quickly became a dear friend and has proven to be a mentor and influencer throughout our entire movement. Today when I ask our people around the world about how God spoke to them about the future, many of them mention Joe Ewen. Through his incredible prophetic ministry, he has consistently offered words from the Lord, deeply touching us with healing in our personal lives and empowerment for our futures.

In Banff, Joe encouraged our group to go out in the city to share God's message of love and hope. During one of our morning times of prayer, I was asking God where we should go to start that day's outreach. I asked everyone to pray and ask God to show them, and we would go out from there. God gave me an image of a horseshoe and a bar. When I asked one of the Scottish men if there was a place like that nearby, he directed me to the Horseshoe Bar on High Street. I followed the man's directions, found the place, and walked in.

"Excuse me!" I said loudly to get everyone's attention. "Could I take a few minutes of your time to tell you how much Jesus loves you and how you can know Him?"

As you might imagine, no one seemed particularly interested. But I shared anyway. When I was finished, one guy waved me over. We went to a side booth, and he told me his story: the night before, he had tried to kill himself. Just as he had taken a knife to his throat, though, an invisible hand stopped him and caused him to crumple to his knees. This experience made him think that God existed, but he didn't know how to know God.

When he finished his story, I shared how he could know Jesus personally. He came to faith right there. His girlfriend eventually gave her life to Jesus, too, and they both got involved in the church and were later married.

God Will Make a Way

In the third summer of our discipleship school, the outreach was planned for Thailand. Laura and I were going with the team, but this time we were also taking our new baby girl. Since birth, Abby had suffered with colic. Needless to say, several people in our lives, including some family members, were not happy about our decision to take a frail five-month-old to a developing country.

We knew that Abby would have to get her second round of routine immunizations while we were there. We already knew that the hospital in Thailand had the shots she would need, and we went there as scheduled. As is often the case, she had a slight reaction, which developed into a high fever.

Our team was scheduled to travel from Bangkok to a rural orphanage in the northern part of Thailand and into nearby villages to share Christ. We decided that Laura should stay back until Abby was better and then fly up later with one of the host missionaries. When the team reached the orphanage, we discovered there had been an outbreak of measles. I called Laura to tell her what was happening. Abby's fever was gone, but we agreed to pray that night and then talk the next morning to decide what to do.

The next morning I called Laura, fully expecting her to stay in Bangkok. But she had stayed up most of the night reading a memoir of Rosalind Goforth, a missionary who risked her life and her children's lives for the sake of seeing the gospel reach the unreached. Laura said God used the story to empower her and give her the faith to join us. God had spoken these words to her: *I will take care of you and Abby. Trust Me.* He didn't say it would be free from trials, but He would be present. That evening Laura arrived at the orphanage, crying baby in tow. We spent the first of many nights swatting mosquitoes off of Abby while she slept.

Rose, the woman who ran the orphanage, had taken children in from all over northern Thailand. As they got older she prayed with them about going back to their home villages to preach the gospel. One of those young men wanted to take us to a village that, to his knowledge, had never heard that message.

It took a full day just to get to a village where we were stopping at a midway point. That night we slept on mats in homes that sat on stilts above the pigs and livestock. The conditions were difficult for us all, and Laura and I wondered, *Did we do the right thing?*

Miracles in the Nations

When we shared the gospel in that village the next morning, we saw an encouraging response, but there were still a few more hours of rough travel to our final destination. When we finally arrived, the men were in the fields. In that culture the women would not listen to us until the men were present, so we waited.

While we waited for the men to get home, Jeff, a student in the discipleship school, began to sing "Jesus Loves Me." The children began to sing back in what sounded like perfect English in perfect pitch. Because Thai is a tonal language, they were able to sing even if they didn't understand all the words. Jeff kept singing, and they kept repeating. Jesus loves me ... *Jesus loves me* ... this I know ... *this I know* ... for the Bible tells me so ... *for the Bible tells me so* ... .

Jeff stood up and walked through the village continuing to sing as a crowd of children followed behind. Yes, Jesus loves me ... *Yes, Jesus loves me*. We spent the afternoon singing songs, praising God, and inviting His presence among us.

When the men returned that evening, Dave, our missionary host, shared the gospel with those who gathered. The best we know, as darkness set in, all the people of the village—every one—got on their knees and gave their lives to Christ. The cost was great, but God honored the sacrifice and kept Abby safe.

Laura and I have seen through the years that simply listening to and obeying God, no matter the cost, always bears the greatest fruit. I'm thankful to walk through life with a woman who has a heart to say yes to Jesus.

Oh, by the way, Abby arrived back in Bangkok healthier than when she left. God is good.

> JESUS CAME WITH A MESSAGE OF LOVE, FORGIVENESS, AND POWER. WHEN WE BOLDLY PREACH THE GOSPEL, PRAY FOR THE SICK, AND LOVE PEOPLE IN THEIR BROKENNESS, THAT SAME POWER WILL SHOW UP IN OUR LIVES AND THE LIVES OF OTHERS.

CHAPTER 7

WHY COLLEGE STUDENTS?

In place of your fathers will be your sons;
You shall make them princes in all the earth.

PSALM 45:16

"Jimmy, I'd like for you to pray about being the college pastor." It was February of 1990, and I was sitting in our pastor's office as he made his request. I thought to myself, *Well, I can't think of anything less desirable than that.* From my perspective, college students just wanted to party, play games, and watch movies. I wanted to train Navy Seals for Jesus. On top of that, the pastor had just fired three of the elders who were friends and mentors to Laura and me. We were already thinking God might be leading us elsewhere. But Laura and I determined a long time ago that God had full permission to lead our lives. It was time to seek Him.

While the discipleship students went off to Mexico for their spring break mission trip, Laura and I stayed home to fast and pray. After seven days of fasting, I heard nothing. Frustrated, I went for a walk and told God, "Lord, I'm hungry, and You're not speaking to me. I have to hear from You. I need to give an answer to the pastor. Would You please say something?"

Then a thought entered my mind: *Maybe you're asking the wrong question.*

"Lord," I said, immediately, "am I asking the wrong question?"

Immediately He responded, "Are you in this for Me and My Kingdom, or for you and yours?"

"Lord, we've sacrificed everything and sold all we had," I replied. "Of course I'm in this for Your Kingdom."

Have you ever noticed that if God asks a question, He already knows the answer? I realized I had been thinking about what was best for me, not what was best for Him. I was fasting, but I did so wanting God to tell me what I wanted to hear. So I prayed, "Lord, whatever is best for You and Your Kingdom, I'll do it."

I heard Him say: *If you will stay, I will raise up people to start churches all over the world. I've asked you to lead them and be a part of this. Stay and watch Me work.*

That was enough for me. I ran home to Laura, and she was in total agreement. If God was calling us to lead the college ministry, we would stay in Waco.

After I accepted the college pastor position, I began to research movements of God among college students. I found that they were the catalysts to major revivals of God, not only in American history but also in world history. In 1806, five students from Williams College in Massachusetts met in a grove of trees near campus to pray. They took shelter under a haystack during a thunderstorm, but they continued to pray that God would send them to share the gospel with the unreached. That time of prayer ignited a movement of God among college students across America, and it was the catalyst for a missionary movement to the nations.

In the 1880s, a missionary movement started in England when a small group of college students at Cambridge and Oxford were stirred by God's heart for the unreached in China. Eventually, they would share with college students all over the East Coast of America, which stirred personal renewal and fire for Jesus and a willingness to do anything for His name to be known in all the earth. Over the next forty years, half of those who were sent out as missionaries from America came from what would be called the Student Volunteer Movement for Foreign Missions.

In 1970, God moved powerfully at Asbury College in Wilmore, Kentucky. This deep move of repentance would spread to college campuses from New

York to California and to churches across America. God often chose to show up among college students who were hungry and willing to do whatever He would ask! These stories, among others, stirred Laura and me to believe that He could do the same thing again with our college students. We were excited to be a part of this legacy.

A Team Gathers

We first formed foundations with the college ministry by meeting with twenty-three men and women whom Laura and I had invested in and spent time with over the years. They came to us at different times to say, "We're in. How can we serve? How can we do this together?"

We spent time fasting and praying together as a team on Sundays. We would then meet in the afternoons for two to three hours. During the first hour, we would worship and pray. During the second hour, we discussed key questions: How do we do small groups? How do we teach people to pray? *How* do we connect people to the lost of the world? Gathering with this early leadership team, seeking the Lord,and ministering together was the seedbed for a tightly knit community model of church life.

In those times together we mapped out a process to involve every student in prayer, small groups, and missions. We believed God wanted us to train young men and women to change the world throughout their lives, not just during their college years.

As we prayed and waited on the Lord during this time, God gave us Psalm 45:16: "In place of your fathers will be your sons. You shall make them princes in all the earth." Our leadership team realized that if we would invest in young men and women, then they would become leaders in the Kingdom. They would be used mightily by the Lord to change the world.

Another encouraging foundational piece came through a sophomore at Baylor named Jeff Abshire. After we explained the college pastor transition to the student leadership team, Jeff walked up to me and said, "You know, this is hard for me because I really love our current college pastor, Mark. I have been thankful for his leadership, but God has put it in my heart to serve you. I am here to love, encourage, and practically serve you in every way I can. You just let me know, and I am here for you."

That was more than twenty years ago. In a lifetime, there are rarely people who come along and complement you perfectly. Jeff has served as my right arm throughout all these years (and by the way, I am left handed). Every movement needs vision and implementation. God brought Jeff early on to facilitate and administrate the things that God had put in our hearts. Jeff's model of faithful, loving service has invited hundreds of others with similar gifts to do the same. Jesus said He came to serve and not to be served, and Jeff has followed that model for our movement over and over again. Antioch would not be what it is without him and others with servant hearts.

Beginning with Prayer

Jeremiah 29:11–13 says, "'For I know the plans I have for you,' declares the Lord, 'plans for welfare and not for calamity to give you a future and a hope that you will call upon Me and pray to Me and I will listen to you. You will seek Me and find Me when you search for Me with your whole heart and I will be found by you.'" What a beautiful, clear passage about how to enter into God's destiny for our lives.

God has great plans for each of us, but His promises are tied to our calling out to Him through prayer and submitting our lives to Him. As a group, we knew we needed to train students both to understand the sovereignty of God and how to partner with Him to see His purposes fulfilled. We began with prayer.

We did this in every way we could think of. We created structured outlines to help students study the Word, worship, and pray each day. But we knew it would not be enough to simply give instructions—it would have to be modeled. We sat in apartments and dorm rooms with three or four students at a time so they could watch the way we read the Word, worshipped, and prayed. We would pray out loud, read the Word out loud, and worship together. After a few days together students were ready to do it on their own. Teaching students how to have a life-giving devotional time would be the centerpiece for their personal transformation and the empowerment they would need to do the will of God.

We also taught students to pray corporately. People often dislike prayer meetings because they don't feel like God actually hears and answers their prayers. They give general requests about grandma's health, somebody's hurt leg, or prayer for a test, and then someone prays for the list. Often there is no sense of agreement or of becoming part of God's mission together.

In order to change the "stale prayer meeting" paradigm, we started Early Morning Prayer (EMP), joining together at 6:00 a.m. in campus apartments. At the start of each meeting, students shared how God had answered prayers from the previous week. That stirred faith in the room! We would worship through two or three songs to engage with God and then gather into groups of two or three to pray together. We had adopted the motto "A prayer meeting is not a prayer meeting unless every person prays." In order to facilitate this, smaller groups of pray-ers were vital to getting everyone involved. At times, to help people learn to pray, we provided outlines describing what we were believing God for in specific lives, in the college ministry, and in the nations.

We would often close these meetings with "rally cry" prayers. One person would lead out, and everyone would join in with one voice. There was more excitement about attending prayer meetings than any other gathering in our ministry. We even had reports of people bringing friends who didn't know Jesus—and who came to know the Lord in the middle of our prayer meetings.

We also taught people how to pray in their Lifegroup. At the end of every Lifegroup gathering, students would break up into groups of three and pray for one another's needs as well as for a friend to either come to faith in Jesus or to come back to Jesus.

One night in particular, a group of students was in an apartment praying. One of the students, who lived next door, was praying for her roommate. The walls were thin, and that roommate was actually on the other side of the wall listening. This young woman was a partier who, up to that point, had wanted nothing to do with God or His people. She heard that group calling her name out before God, saying,

"Lord, would You visit Lane? God would you convict her of sin? God, would you bring her to You? You know her heart is hurting. She needs you."

Lane was on her bed, sitting against the wall. She explains that a presence came over her, and she began to cry uncontrollably. She suddenly realized that God loved her and that she had been living a life of sin, and it was time to turn toward God.

She wasn't sure what to do, but she knew she had to do something. She jumped off her bed, headed next door, and knocked on the door. Eventually somebody opened the door.

"I am Lane. I am the girl you all are praying for. I live next door. I need Jesus," she said.

Lane gave her life to Jesus, and during her last two years of college she was deeply involved with our ministry, leading and discipling others in the ways of Jesus.

Discipleship in Lifegroups

We knew that we were called to train college men and women to do church and community in such a way that it could be reproduced anywhere in the world. As we studied the Scriptures we kept coming back to Acts 2:42–47:

"They were continually devoting themselves to the apostles' teaching and to fellowship, to the breaking of bread and to prayer. Everyone kept feeling a sense of awe; and many wonders and signs were taking place through the apostles. And all those who had believed were together and had all things in common; and they began selling their property and possessions and were sharing them with all, as anyone might have need. Day by day continuing with one mind in the temple, and break-ing bread from house to house, they were taking their meals together with gladness and sincerity of heart, praising God and having favor with all the people. And the Lord was adding to their number day by day those who were being saved."

All the elements of church life are in that passage: pastoral care, Bible teaching, connecting people to one another, sharing meals together, God's demonstrating His power, and people being added to the church daily.

Small-group experiences are often based just on fellowship and pastoral care. These are important elements, but God also intends for our gatherings to be a base for missional community. So we incorporated evangelism and discipleship as components to our Lifegroups, helping the groups grow and multiply in order to see the Kingdom of God advance.

Honestly we all would say those first groups were pretty boring and at times, embarrassing. But we continued to learn, and slowly but surely we saw people helped, restored, and empowered to follow God. The key to successful Lifegroups was discipleship: intentionally investing in a person's life so he or she can in turn invest in another person's life. People would meet in groups of two or three and ask the "3 Big Questions":

1. How is your devotional life and how can I help you?

2. Is there any sin in your life that you need to confess?

3. Who are you reaching out to and how can I help you do that better?

Developing a small-group movement was completely dependent on the strength of our discipleship. Nothing paid more significant returns for our college ministry than our perseverance with intentional discipleship—one person investing in another with the expectation of continuing that pattern.

Mansour's Story

The second key piece for our small groups to remain missional was a focus on intentional evangelism. We encouraged small groups to work together as a team to pray for, become friends with, and share with those who didn't know Jesus. Amazing things happened when students followed these simple disciplines.

One Lifegroup had a heart for international students, especially Muslim students. That year, Mansour was a freshman from the Middle East attending Baylor. Guys from the Lifegroup befriended Mansour, loving him and including him in their lives. He ate meals with them, played soccer with them, and eventually even came to church and Lifegroup with them. As a Muslim from a very devout family, Mansour had no intention of responding to the gospel, but he enjoyed their friendship and love. The Lifegroup prayed for him and many times even took a day to fast and pray for him, too.

After several months of hanging with our guys, Mansour realized he had to make a decision for or against this Jesus. He began to pull back and told Josh, the leader of the Lifegroup, that although he loved them, it was becoming awkward. Mansour was not willing to come to Christ, but he saw that Jesus was a huge part of their lives. He didn't know what to do, so he backed off to reevaluate how he should relate to his friends.

When Mansour pulled away, though, our guys didn't. They didn't pressure him, but they prayed all the more asking God to break through. One night, Mansour knocked at Josh's door around 2:00 a.m. "I have had a couple of dreams this week about Jesus," he said, "but the one tonight shook me so much that I had to talk to you. In the dream, there was a holy man asking who I knew with names that begin with the letter J. I started naming people I knew—Josh, Jennifer, Jessica, Jacob, Jerry, and so on—until I got to ten names, but he was looking for eleven names. The man said to me, 'One is missing. This one is the most important one for all eternity and all the ages. This is the one you must know.' I knew it was Jesus, and I called out to Him."

Mansour went on to ask Josh, "What do I do from here?"

Josh had been studying the Qur'an in order to relate to and understand Mansour's world. He felt if God were speaking to Mansour, he would let go of Islam. So Josh put the Qur'an in Mansour's hand and told him to put it behind his back, pray to receive Jesus, and then set down the Qur'an and walk away from it. Mansour prayed a simple prayer of devotion to Christ and a commitment to have no other gods before Him. He set down the Qur'an and walked out of the room a different man.

Mansour was established and strengthened the last couple of months before he left school to return home to the Middle East. Josh and the others sent a Bible with Mansour which he hid in his room behind a dresser. One of the family's housekeepers found it a couple of months later and took it to his father. Mansour's father was outraged and threatened to beat and disown him.

Mansour found a way to get in touch with our guys and asked, "What do I do? My father will not allow me to email you anymore. I cannot communicate with you. Pray for me. Please pray for me."

The guys didn't hear from him for about thirty days. When he was able to contact them again, he said his father had taken him out of Baylor and sent him to another university in the Middle East. Mansour asked if we knew anyone in that country who knew Jesus. We were able to connect him with some people from another organization who began to disciple him, love him, and care for him. As of our last conversation, Mansour was loving and serving Jesus and walking with Him.

Spring Break Missions

Matthew 24:14 says, "This gospel of the kingdom shall be preached in the whole world as a testimony to all the nations, and then the end will come." Throughout history, this passage has been the rallying cry for students to believe for the evangelization of the world in their generation. We gain a great sense of purpose in our lives when we have a cause greater than ourselves to live and to die for. Our college students needed something more to live for than being good, getting a job, and pursuing the American dream. So we preached and taught and told stories of God's heart for the nations, and most importantly, we facilitated ways they could touch the nations themselves. One of the ways we did this was through short-term mission trips.

Every spring break we took college students to Mexico. They would experience firsthand how to share the gospel on the streets, care for the poor, pray for the sick, and communicate cross-culturally. Every morning we gathered for worship, prayer, and teaching that would call students to surrender everything to Jesus. In the afternoons and evenings, we worked with local churches to reach out in their communities all over the city. These were times when students not only heard the call to missions but also experienced it firsthand.

Marci, 1999

One of our college students describes the impact of her first spring break trip:

My freshman year of college, I knew nothing about the power of the Holy Spirit or sharing boldly with the lost. I went on the Juarez, Mexico, trip ripe for change.

Every morning, we would spend one hour with God alone and then gather together for corporate worship. These times were power-ful as I learned to hear the voice of God speak to me and prepare me for the events each day. We would wait on God to reveal words or pictures of people He wanted us to share with or minister to that day. I was so surprised to hear God so clearly in the morning about things that would happen in the afternoon.

Once, we got a picture of a woman in need of healing. We prayed for her healing before we went out. Later, as we were doing an outreach, we saw the woman we had pictured earlier and shared with her. She wanted to accept the truth of Jesus, and we prayed for her to be healed. God healed her of stomach problems.

On another morning in prayer God gave us great faith for many to be saved that night. After the outreach that night, we real-ized that a hundred people gave their lives to Jesus.

These experiences of seeing people so hungry to know Jesus and immediately accepting Him broke my heart for people who have never heard about Him. As I watched masses gather around us to hear the gospel, many of them decided to follow God. My heart stirred and came alive. I knew this was what God wants us to do all the time, wherever we are.

The spring break trip taught me what God expects from my daily life with Him: to spend time with Him and to minister all day out of a place of intimacy with Him. We should listen to His voice for ourselves and others so they can see how much God cares about them personally.

These experiences would not only continue annually during spring break, but they would also carry over into short-term trips all over the world each summer. We have sent thousands of students to more than eighty nations to be a part of God's heart for fulfilling Matthew 24:14.

Prayer, Lifegroups, and missions. God had given us a strategy and a plan to reach college students and help them become empowered to change the world in whatever location or vocation He would lead them to. Even today those basics still fuel hundreds of Antioch college students who gather week by week to pursue their passion for Jesus and His purposes in the earth.

The Savills' Story

Sara Savill came to Baylor University in August 2002 and quickly got involved in a Lifegroup at Antioch. She dove in with all her heart and eventually led her own Lifegroup.

In August of 2004 Sara's sister, Shelly, transferred to Baylor to start her sophomore year. Shelly had been making disastrous life choices—partying, drugs, alcohol—but she hoped that moving to Waco would help her start a new life. Shortly after transferring to Baylor, though, she found herself headed in the same old direction.

Sara's heart broke for her sister, as did the hearts of many friends in her community. At one point some of their Lifegroup community felt the Holy Spirit impressing on them that Shelly was in danger. She was at the crossroads of making a decision between continuing down a path that would lead to her death or choosing a path toward life in Jesus. So the entire Lifegroup decided to fast on Shelly's behalf.

Things did not look hopeful when Shelly showed up at the Lifegroup leader's apartment and announced in a belligerent and scornful manner that she would never accept Jesus. "I know I'm going to hell," Shelly said, "and I'm fine with that."

Although brokenhearted, Sara and the Lifegroup continued to believe God for Shelly's life. Shelly seemed to take a turn for the worse when she and her boyfriend broke up. She threw herself fully into drugs and stopped eating and sleeping. She seemed to be bent on destroying her life, but during a drug-induced high, Shelly mysteriously began talking with a friend about Jesus and how He was the only way to heaven. The more she talked, the more she convinced herself. Eventually she looked at her friend through tears and said, "God is giving me another chance. I would be a fool not to accept His offer of a changed life."

On that day, September 25, 2005, Shelly left her apartment and went straight to Sara's place. Sara opened the door, shocked to find her sister standing there—broken, tenderhearted, and ready to give her life to the Lord. The Lifegroup celebrated that night as word quickly spread that God had intervened when things seemed most hopeless. The next week at our college service, the celebration rivaled that of a football national championship game.

Shelly's parents, Byron and Liz, were so touched by their daughter's transformation that they moved to Waco to attend Antioch's discipleship training school. After finishing, they joined the staff and moved to Nagano City, Japan, where they still serve as missionaries. Sara became deeply involved in serving with the urban ministries of Antioch. After going through the training school, she joined a church-planting team in India, which she and her husband, Bill, now lead.

Shelly became a Lifegroup leader, discipling young women. She spent a summer in Peru, where she was able to boldly share her testimony of God's deliverance, and she led many people to the Lord. After attending the discipleship school in 2009, Shelly moved to Seattle to work with an Antioch church-planting team in the city. She and her husband, Garrett, are now on a team that is starting a new Antioch church in Edmonds, Washington.

Shelly and her entire family are being used powerfully by God to see lives transformed as they serve Him with all their hearts. They have become reconciled to one another and are growing fully in love with Jesus. This all began because a group of college students believed Acts 2:42-47 was intended to be lived out today.

WHEN STUDENTS ENCOUNTER JESUS AND HIS TRANSFORMING POWER, THEY ARE READY TO CHANGE THE WORLD. HOWEVER, THAT EXCITEMENT NEEDS A PROCESS TO GET THEM THERE. THE CHURCH IS THAT ANSWER.

CHAPTER 8

REVIVAL FROM THE INSIDE OUT

Therefore repent and return, so that your sins may be wiped away,
in order that times of refreshing may come from the presence of the Lord.

ACTS 3:19

When Laura and I began leading the college ministry, we started off boldly. My first message? "Revival or Nothing"!

Here's the thing: God wants to do a great work through us, but before He can do that, He has to do a great work in us. I knew from both church history and personal experience we needed God to touch us in such a powerful way that we would be forever changed.

At the church at Antioch in the book of Acts, we see that the Lord was moving powerfully, but before God was to launch them into the world, they were preparing the way through prayer and fasting. Acts 13:2-3 says, "While they were ministering to the Lord and fasting, the Holy Spirit said, 'Set apart for Me Barnabas and Saul for the work to which I have called them.' Then, when they had fasted and prayed and laid their hands on them, they sent them away." That would begin the Spirit-empowered, world-changing missionary journeys of Paul.

I feel I need to confess here that fasting is not the easiest discipline for me. I like food, and I have to think that I may just get a greater reward in heaven because it's harder for me than everybody else. (Okay, I know that's not true, but the point is it's hard.) Still, we knew that we needed to fast and pray as a group. During those early years, especially between 1990 and 1992, it seemed that not a month went by when we didn't organize a three-day, prayer-filled fast. During those three days we would have different groups of students praying every hour over those seventy-two hours, calling out to God.

We also challenged people individually to fast and pray for their friends and neighbors because we needed to unlock the power of God. Something had to happen beyond what we had known, beyond the status quo. Based on Scripture readings and history lessons, we knew we had to go beyond simply praying and believing. Emptying ourselves and depending fully on God would open us to the fullness of God.

But there were some low days during those seasons. Discouraged, I went to a mentor one day and asked, "Is this really working? We've got a great process. We've got students doing discipleship and evangelism. We're experiencing a measure of God's presence. But is the fasting really working or even needed?"

I've held onto his response. He said, "You know, everybody will jump on the bandwagon once God is moving, but you'll have that privilege of knowing you were part of the journey that unlocked the door. You can't get that kind of intimacy with Jesus any other way."

Those words were enough to keep us going. By the fall of 1992, about 150 students were gathering corporately and getting involved in Lifegroups. We were planting our first churches overseas, and our students were engaged in meaningful summer outreaches. It was all rich and it was right—but something was still missing.

Then, unexpectedly, something happened. During a leadership meeting that fall, about forty students were gathered. As we worshipped, one of the students said, "I believe I have a word from God for us as a group." She went on to share Hosea 6:4: "What shall I do with you, O Ephraim? What shall I do with you, O Judah? For your loyalty is like a morning cloud and like the dew which goes away early."

The student continued, "We are to return to our first love and not be like the dew on the ground." Then she began to weep uncontrollably. Suddenly, we all began to weep, realizing we hadn't given Jesus our *whole* hearts. We wanted to do great works for Jesus. We wanted to be a part of what He was doing in the world. And we wanted to be a part of the exciting stories of miracles. But did we really want *Jesus*? Was He the all-consuming passion of our lives?

That leaders' meeting, which was scheduled for an hour, went on for three and a half hours, and the power of it wasn't only in that first word. After about an hour, another girl walked up to me shaking with fear and said, "I have to share something. I have to share something."

I asked softly, "What is it? Are you okay?"

"I had an abortion when I was in high school," she said quietly. "I never told anybody. I have to say it to everyone."

Okay, God is into humility, but not humiliation. Is this really right? I wondered.

But in that moment, as a pastor and leader, I knew it was okay. She was among family and friends who wouldn't condemn her, and she wasn't trying to get attention. So she shared.

"Many of you know me as a nice person, and I try to be that," she began. "But in high school I got involved in relationships out of my own neediness, and I got pregnant. My mom slipped me off to an abortion clinic, and I've never told anyone. I need help. Jesus, please help me."

Well, we were all undone. We gathered around her and prayed for her. Then someone else tapped me on the shoulder and said, "I need to share something, too."

Over the next two hours, others shared current struggles and past sins. You have to remember that in the early 1990s, this was not a normal part of church. Sin was associated with shame, and these things were rarely talked about, let alone confessed publicly. With each person who shared, though, the presence of God increased. I went home that night grieving the pain in people's lives but rejoicing that they had felt free enough to be open about their brokenness.

When I got home I asked, "God, what do I do?" He led me to find my old journal. Five years earlier, I read through the Bible and created my own concordance in that journal. So I spent time looking up the verses I had recorded on getting free from sin. As I did, I noticed a pattern in Scripture for gaining freedom from sin: confession, repentance, the Word of God, and ministering out of our brokenness.

That next Sunday morning, at our weekly corporate gathering, I began a series called "Freedom from Sin." I started talking about the power of confession and God's desire to forgive and cleanse, and then I emphasized the need to get honest with God and others. I shared my own junk from the past and how I had hoped no one would ever find out. These things had been hurtful to God, others, and me. You could have heard a pin drop in the place.

After I finished, I invited people forward to pray and confess. For two hours, people poured out their hearts to the leaders who were waiting for them at the front. We prayed for them, and they would fall into a heap, experiencing God's forgiveness and love like never before. It was amazing. It was terrible. It was wonderful. It was revival.

Finding Freedom from Sin

Before we could fully experience God's power in our lives, we had to empty ourselves. These are the elements we emphasized:

CONFESSION: In 1 John 1:9, we read, "If we confess our sins, He is faithful and righteous to forgive us our sins and to cleanse us from all unrighteousness." Confession literally means to agree with God, to see sin as God sees it, and to own it. Confession brings freedom. When sins that were hidden in the dark are brought to light, the enemy loses his power. He can no longer harass us and keep us bound with secret fears—*What if someone found out? What if people really knew about me?* The enemy can use that kind of shame like a ball and chain that yanks us around, but once the chain is broken, we can find true freedom.

Confession is the beginning of real repentance, which causes real revival, which causes real transformation. It's not simply about being blessed—it's about being set free.

REPENTANCE: If confession is opening the door to God's light and power, then repentance is closing the door to future sin. This is how 2 Corinthians 7:9-11 explains it:

"I now rejoice, not that you were made sorrowful, but that you were made sorrowful to the point of repentance; for you were made sorrowful according to the will of God, so that you might not suffer loss in anything through us. For the sorrow that is according to the will of God produces a repentance without regret, leading to salvation, but the sorrow of the world produces death. For behold what earnestness this very thing, this godly sorrow, has produced in you: what vindication of yourselves, what indignation, what fear, what longing, what zeal, what avenging of wrong! In everything you demonstrated yourselves to be innocent in the matter."

The idea isn't, *I got caught, so now I'll confess.* It's, *I want to do whatever it takes to be free forever.* That is repentance.

We also offered practical steps to help people in their journeys of repentance. The first was to make restitution for every wrong done. People were calling past girlfriends and boyfriends to ask for forgiveness. They were going to their parents, asking for forgiveness for lies, rebellion, and stealing. We had people, as I had done myself, writing letters to companies or people they had worked for to right wrongs and make financial restitution for times when they had stolen. We were not just confessing our sins—we were repenting and closing the door so those sins would no longer have power over us.

In particular, one graduate student started off, as others had, by saying, "I never told this to anyone." He began talking about his involvement in occult activities through Dungeons and Dragons, a role-playing game that was popular at that time. As he continued, he confessed to some of the most extreme demonic, sexual perversion I had ever heard in one setting. Once he opened the door, it all just came out. He said he actually felt lighter physically, like a huge burden had been lifted. As we talked about staying free, I asked him to pray about what needed to change.

He went home and pulled out the occult books, the perverse books, and anything that was not of God. He took it all to the middle of a field, made a big pile, and held his own bonfire in the middle of the night. He declared, "I am done with it all!" It was like a scene straight out of Acts 19:19-20: "And many of those who practiced magic brought their books together and began burning them. … So the word of the Lord was growing mightily and prevailing."

That man is older now. He has served the Lord faithfully and has honored God in his marriage and in the lives of his children. He has served the Lord around the world. It began with confession *and* action-oriented repentance.

BUILDING UP IN THE WORD: Scripture warns in Luke 11:24-26 that if you clean your house and leave it empty, the enemy will come back and bring his friends. So what do we use to fill the gap after confession and repentance? The Word of God.

The classic foundation we go over again and again are Jesus' words to His disciples: "And you will know the truth, and the truth will make you free" (John 8:32). Without the Word of God, the work of God in a person's life isn't sustainable.

As we coached people in studying God's Word, finding Scriptures related to their personal brokenness or need, we also knew we needed a practical tool to help them. At that time, Neil T. Anderson came out with his second book, titled *The Bondage Breaker*. At the end, he included a prayer process called the "7 Steps to Freedom." One on one, we took students through a detailed process of renunciation of evil and the truth of God's Word, followed by affirmation from the Bible that would strengthen them and establish them in God's grace. We have taken thousands of people through those steps as part of their journey to wholeness.

MINISTRY OUT OF BROKENNESS: Confession, repentance, and the Word of God are followed by being unashamed to minister out of our brokenness. God gives us victory in our lives that goes beyond ourselves. If we receive freedom from God and are then unwilling to help rescue others, then we become stagnant pools instead of the rivers of life that God intended. Every time we share our story, we set another person free to do the same. Our greatest place of brokenness can become our greatest place of ministry if we let God do His work in us.

Long before God birthed Antioch Community Church, He was laying a foundation through the college ministry and the discipleship training school. God's empowering didn't come in the way I expected—it came through a deep work of repentance and emptying of ourselves. Once we were open, we could be used for church planting around the world. God began to burden us not only with prayers for the nations, but also a willingness to go—no matter the cost.

Looking Back

Recently I ran across a photograph from our 1992 spring break mission trip. There are 150 people in that picture, and I still know where almost all of these people are. Most of them are all still serving God in some way, and that kind of result comes only through revival from the inside out.

When we talk about revival, many times we think of it as some big, sweeping event. But it doesn't have to look like that. What I've found is if we are following the habits of confession, repentance, building up in the Word, and ministering to others, then we can live in revival. Revival isn't a moment. It's a lifestyle for those who choose it. We can be made new—revived—every day.

> REVIVAL BEGINS WITH REPENTANCE.
> REPENTANCE OPENS THE WAY FOR GOD TO FULFILL
> HIS PROMISES THROUGH HIS PEOPLE.

CHAPTER 9

DREAM YOUR DREAMS

*And thus I aspired to preach the gospel, not where Christ was
already named, so that I would not build on another man's foundation;
but as it is written, "They who had no news of Him shall see,
and they who have not heard shall understand."*

ROMANS 15:20-21

In 1991, I went to visit Fuller Seminary in California for a few days to learn how to train church planters. While I was there, a man I didn't know walked over to me and said he felt impressed by God to give me a Scripture passage. He handed me a scrap of paper with Isaiah 54:2–3 written on it. I thanked him, tucked it away in my pocket, and went on my way, planning to read it later.

A couple of days later, I was back in Waco when Kurt, a dear friend who has served with us overseas, came to me to say he had been praying for me all week. He also told me that God had led him to give me the Scripture Isaiah 54:2–3.

At 6:00 a.m. the next morning, my friend Joe Ewen called from Scotland. He said, "Jimmy, I have been praying for you, and God told me to call you this morning and give you this Scripture: Isaiah 54:2–3."

Now, I may not always hear the Lord well, but I knew that this time God was speaking directly to me—and to us as a people. As I opened my Bible, I was stunned by the words and promise of God in Isaiah 54:2-3:

"Enlarge the place of your tent;
   Stretch out the curtains of your dwellings, spare not;
   Lengthen your cords and strengthen your pegs.
   For you will spread abroad to the right and to the left.
   And your descendants will possess nations
   And will resettle the desolate cities."

This passage came to me during a time I was working through how to discern whether we were following God's desires or our own. I had started to pray this prayer:

God, dream your dreams through me. If there is something out there that nobody else wants to do, something no one else will do, something You are thinking about in heaven that You want to get done and You want a vessel, then dream Your dreams through me—and not just through me, but dream Your dreams through us.

God had already spoken to our team about church planting, but He was making it clear that we were to focus on planting churches in countries where people have never heard the gospel. God was calling us as a people to believe Him for even greater things, to continue to branch out by faith, and to trust Him to do above and beyond what we could ask or imagine. He wanted us to reach desolate cities to the left and the right, places where people have never heard the gospel before. He wanted us to reach the unreached.

So those of us involved in the discipleship training school decided to begin phase two of our vision to send out long-term church planters. We offered discipleship school graduates the opportunity to take four months of training in the fall and then be sent out to plant a church somewhere in the world—we weren't sure where. Four people responded, and we all took a step of blind faith, believing God would support us and show us the way.

That summer we sent teams to explore possibilities from Asia to Europe. Our eventual team leader, Ben Cox, felt God was telling him we were supposed to plant where Europe and Asia meet and then minister to both Asians and Europeans. He explored Asia while I took a group to Eastern Europe.

An Angel in a VW Van

At the end of the Cold War, Eastern Europe was an open, ripe harvest field. In the summer of 1991, Laura, Abby, our discipleship school team of thirteen, and I headed to Eastern Europe for our summer outreach. The journey proved to be a determining marker in our lives.

After spending a couple of weeks working with a local church in Germany, we began a trek down to Veliko Tarnovo, Bulgaria. The man who had connected us with a pastor in Veliko Tarnovo gave us a map and directions for how to get there, which went something like this: go south from Munich to Vienna. Take a right and go to Szeged, Hungary. Take the road to Belgrade, Yugoslavia, and then go straight south to Sophia, Bulgaria. Finally, head back west toward Varna and the Mediterranean Sea. Veliko Tarnovo is on that road.

Those directions led to some interesting adventures. Outside of Belgrade, someone broke into our van, and our backpacks and possessions were strewn everywhere. We had also unwittingly arrived in Yugoslavia just before the outbreak of a series of civil wars that would change the shape of a nation. Throughout the night we heard gunshots and were obviously anxious to head out of town the next morning. After fixing our broken window, we headed out of Belgrade toward Sophia. Of course, we weren't the only ones who'd heard the gunfire, and we found ourselves in the middle of a massive traffic jam as thousands of people were fleeing.

As far as we could see on the main highway, cars were lined up to escape the country. Between our two vans, we talked on walkie-talkies about what we

Dream Your Dreams

should do. We could see that the fence had been cut in a certain section, and we wondered if we should go off the shoulder and through that gap. If we did, though, we would have no idea where to go from there.

Suddenly, when we were almost to a stop, a VW van weaved through the traffic in front of us. The driver stuck his head out the window and waved for us to follow him. No sooner had we asked the Lord whether we should follow the guy than a "Don't Mess with Texas" bumper sticker on the back of his van came into view. Why in the world would a van in the middle of Yugoslavia have a sticker from our home state? Because it was too unbelievable to be a coincidence, we took it as confirmation that God was leading us to follow him.

The van led us through the opening in the barrier toward some dirt roads. We followed him, weaving through little villages for over two hours until we found ourselves at a city near the Bulgarian border. As we came to an intersection, the van leading us turned left where we needed to turn right. The driver pointed us to the right, waved, and then drove away. When we looked back, he and the van were gone. If we had ever seen an angel, we believed it was then.

We got into Sophia, Bulgaria, at dark and began looping the city, looking for the road to Varna. All we kept seeing were signs that said Bapha. Finally, after two hours of driving around, one of our team members in the back said in his thick Texas accent, "Hey, I've been looking at this map, and you know what? Bapha means Varna. That's the Cyrillic alphabet from the Bulgarian language."

So we got on the road to Bapha and pulled into Veliko Tarnovo, Bulgaria, at 2:00 a.m. Pastor Dimitri and the people of his church met us and took us to their homes.

Signs and Wonders

The next day, I met with Dimitri, and he asked what we could do. I told him, "We do worship, dramas, and dance, and we love to preach the gospel and pray for the sick."

"Do they get healed?" he asked.

"Well, sometimes," I responded. "We can at least give it a try."

"Okay, I will let you try tonight. We will meet at my church."

When we met at his church, there were about seventy people packed into a tiny building. People upstairs pressed their ears to the floor, and others were hanging in the windows. Many people came to Jesus that night. The crowd was so dense that we told the people to put their hands on the place of their body that needed healing as we prayed. Three or four of them cried out saying that the Lord had touched them.

Dimitri thought it went well—so well that the next day he rented out the Pioneer Palace, an old Communist gathering hall in the center of the city. About four hundred people showed up, and I felt led to share about the Father-heart of God with this group who had been kept from the knowledge of God for many years. As I talked about the way God cared for each of them as a father, people began to cry and respond.

At the end we said we would like to pray for the sick. We prayed for a man who had trouble seeing, and he took off his glasses and left them behind because he said his eyes were better. Then a man who was completely blind in one eye came for prayer. As we prayed for him, he was healed, too. When the blind man saw, faith rose in the room, and people clamored for prayer. Many people were touched that day, receiving salvation and healing for their bodies and their broken hearts.

That amazing event opened the door for us to share the gospel daily on the streets of Veliko Tarnovo. Several hundred people would gather as we preached of Jesus and His grace. We would ask people to get on their knees in the streets as a sign of their commitment to give their lives to Him. And then, because the crowds were so thick, we would ask them to simply place their hands on the areas that hurt so we could pray for them.

We saw a tumor leave the chest of a woman right before our eyes. Then an older gentleman with a withered hand asked if I would pray for him. I immediately shared the gospel with him, and he gave his life to Christ. As I prayed for his hand, it began to crack and pop, and I actually saw his withered hand become straight. He raised it in the air and shouted, "Hallelujah!"

It was as if the whole crowd knew what had happened. They began to push forward for us to pray for them, too. People also wanted us to visit their friends and family. After we spent time on the city streets, we went out to surrounding areas. One night in particular someone asked us to pray for an uncle in a village on the edge of town. When we got there we could see red streaks in the man's leg as infection and gangrene were setting in. He had an open sore on the bottom of his foot that looked as if it went all the way to the bone. As he unraveled the wrap on his foot, the smell of rotting flesh almost knocked us over.

"Lord," we asked, "how do we pray?" Immediately we felt the Lord say we needed to lay hands on his foot so he could recover. *Oh my goodness.* I thought. *I don't know if I can do this.* But I had decided a long time ago that if God said it, it was enough for me. So we laid our hands on his gangrenous foot and prayed. Right before our very eyes, green, infected flesh began to turn pinkish and healthy. We could see the wound begin to fill in. It filled halfway as we watched. The streaks went out of his legs. He was being healed right there, but the hole in his foot was still not fully healed. We prayed again but nothing happened.

When we asked, "Lord, what do we do?" we heard Him say that by morning the man would be completely healed. We left him with that word from God, and the next morning we got a call telling us his foot was completely whole.

Things like that were astounding to us. We would gather in the mornings and pinch ourselves to make sure it was real. With such revival happening, the people wanted us to pray with them and minister to them twenty-four hours a day. After a week our team was wiped out. We were physically exhausted and needed a break. I promised them we would finish our outreach at 5:00 p.m. the next day so they could have the remainder of the evening to rest.

As that time drew near, our team began packing up to go to the different places where we were staying. The crowds of people, however, weren't leaving. One of the Bulgarian college students turned to us and asked, "Why are you in such a hurry when people are so hungry for Jesus?"

I will never forget those words. I realized God was pouring out His Spirit and showing His love to people who were spiritually starving. So I replied, "You're right. I repent. We will stay as long as people need help."

I told the team that those who wanted to stay could, and the rest could go home. About five of us stayed and continued to minister. That night was one of the most powerful of our lives. God's presence was so heavy that our translators kept falling down under His power. We literally had to hold them up as they translated for us. As pockets of ten and fifteen people came up at a time, we would share the gospel with them, and they would be saved.

One group in particular was a group of Muslims who came to ask for prayer. As we talked about Jesus, they prayed and gave their lives to Christ. One man began to scream. Not knowing why, I watched him as he threw off his shoes, unwrapped something from his feet, and held wooden blocks in the air. He had been using the blocks to help him walk because he had deformed arches. When he prayed to receive Christ, his arches became straight, and the blocks were no longer needed. I can still see him in my mind, holding up the blocks, shouting, "I'm healed! I'm healed! Jesus healed me and forgave me, and He loves me!"

Sometimes, it's when we are exhausted that God wants to move the most.

First Fruits

We saw the church in Veliko Tarnovo grow to several hundred in those weeks. We then traveled to both Romania and Hungary, where we saw this same scene repeated again and again in places where church planting was once impossible. The team remained in Budapest to continue to minister for the next two weeks, while I boarded a train for Amsterdam. I was still praying about where to send a long-term team.

As I rode all night, I reflected on everything God had done in Bulgaria, Romania, and Hungary. Then I began to think about Russia and wondered what God was doing there. I prayed a simple prayer: "God, if all of this is happening in Eastern Europe, would you show me what's happening in Russia?" I found myself praying that way several times throughout the night.

When I arrived in Amsterdam the next morning, I met my friend Derryck, one of the leaders at the YWAM base there, for breakfast. We had barely said hello when Derryck said, "Let me tell you what God is doing in Russia." It looked as though God was going to answer my prayer for sure.

Derryck told me incredible stories of revival across Russia. They had seen hundreds of people saved through outreaches in many of the larger cities west of the Ural Mountains. At one outreach in Moscow, a concert promoter from Siberia was saved. Afterward he offered to set up an eight-city tour throughout Siberia, Mongolia, China, and Uzbekistan for other teams to come and sing and share this message of Jesus.

As the leaders of YWAM sought the Lord about that opportunity, they believed God gave them a specific plan to partner with churches in North America and Western Europe in the venture. YWAM would present the initial concerts in those cities, and the partner churches would provide laborers to stay behind to plant churches. Derryck explained the vision and offered us a chance to partner with them. After a month of prayer and consulting with our leaders, we agreed that God was leading us to be a part of that new adventure.

YWAM asked us to help plant a church in Ulan-Ude, Siberia, a place where the Buryats, an indigenous group of Asian descent, live in harmony with European Russians. The first fruits of the Isaiah 54:2–3 promise were about to come to pass.

GOD, DREAM YOUR DREAMS THROUGH ME. IF THERE IS SOMETHING OUT THERE THAT NOBODY ELSE WANTS TO DO, SOMETHING NO ONE ELSE WILL DO, SOMETHING YOU ARE THINKING ABOUT IN HEAVEN THAT YOU WANT TO GET DONE AND YOU WANT A VESSEL, THEN DREAM YOUR DREAMS THROUGH ME—AND NOT JUST THROUGH ME, BUT DREAM YOUR DREAMS THROUGH US.

CHAPTER 10

THREE CHURCH PLANTS

Now to Him who is able to do far more abundantly beyond all that
we ask or think, according to the power that works within us,
to Him be the glory in the church and in Christ Jesus to
all generations forever and ever. Amen.

EPHESIANS 3:20-21

"You are not welcome!" the woman screamed at us in Russian from behind the counter. Even though I didn't understand the language, I knew what she was saying. There we sat in the middle of a hotel lobby during a blizzard in southern Siberia, unable to check into the hotel we had been directed to. We were waiting to meet the YWAM Christian rock band from Amsterdam to do an outreach that night. After that, we had planned to stay in the city for three weeks to train and disciple new believers who would be the start of a new church plant. No one told us Ulan-Ude was attached to a military city that was not on the map. It was an arms inspection point for the North Atlantic Treaty Organization (NATO), making the city closed to foreigners.

The City That Didn't Want Us

When the band arrived with their Russian translator and support staff, they showed the hotel clerk that they had confirmed reservations for us for one night, and she was forced to let us stay. We had no idea what we would do the next night, but we went to the outreach concert, trusting God would take care of us. Only a hundred twenty people braved the weather, but thirty of them made decisions to follow Jesus. After prayer and the close of the service, the translator invited those who had made decisions for Christ to come up on the stage. The translator looked at me and said, "Well, they're all yours. What would you like to do?"

The band was leaving the next day, along with their translator, so my first question to the new believers was, "Do you know anybody who speaks English?" One young man said he could ask an English teacher from his college to help. We asked the students to meet us at noon the next day with the teacher.

Back at the hotel I asked the Russian translator what we were supposed to do about staying in the city. He shrugged and said, "As you say in America, it's every man for himself."

We went to bed that night not knowing what the next day would hold. When we woke that morning, we spent some time in prayer, asking God for a translator and a way to stay in the city. We met the English teacher, Julia, at noon. Her English was very good, and she said she would love to help us, but she wanted to let us know she was Buddhist.

"It won't bother us if it won't bother you," we said.

"Great," she said. "Just tell me what to say, and I'll say it."

What a way to start a church plant! We were speaking English to a Buddhist, who was translating our Christian message into Russian. Does God have a sense of humor, or what?

Of course, there was even more fun to be had that day. The woman behind the hotel desk told us, through Julia, that we had until 3:00 p.m. to be out of the room or the staff would throw our things outside into the snow.

We knew God had led us there, so we were going to have to trust Him to take care of us. When we had checked in at the U.S. Embassy in Moscow on the way to Ulan-Ude, they gave us the name of the only other American who would be in Ulan-Ude the same time we were there: Captain Scott Cerrone, U.S. Air Force intelligence officer. At that time, Ulan-Ude was a city of about 350,000 people, and we had no idea where Captain Cerrone was or how to locate him. Since our only option was to find him, though, we had to trust God to lead us to him.

Walking out the front door of the hotel, we prayed, "All right, Holy Spirit, which way do we go?" We all felt He was leading us to the left, so that's where we went. About a hundred yards away, at the next intersection, we asked again, "Okay, Lord, which way do we turn now?" We felt that we were to turn left again, and after walking about three hundred yards, we saw a woman with a big video camera on her shoulder. When we got close enough, we heard the man she was filming say, "This is Captain Scott Cerrone of the U.S. Air Force, signing off."

Overjoyed, we shouted, "Scott Cerrone, it's you!"

We all but tackled him to the ground with our hugs. Overwhelmed, he asked who we were and how we got there, since foreigners weren't supposed to be in Ulan-Ude. As we excitedly explained what we were doing and why we needed help to stay in the city, his suspicions grew. Thankfully, his wife was also there.

"Honey, we need to help them in some way," she said.

Yes, yes, listen to your wife! I thought.

Scott had a scheduled meeting that afternoon with a man who was influential in the defense ministry of the Soviet Union. He told us he would see what he could do and then call around 2:00 p.m. to let us know what happened.

As promised, the phone rang around 2:00 p.m. Scott was downstairs with the man from the defense ministry. After greeting them in the lobby, the man asked in a deep voice and heavy Russian accent, "What do you want?"

I told him we needed to stay in the city for three weeks because we were telling people about God's love and wanted to finish what we had started. After he heard my request, he spoke with the woman who had been screaming at us for the past twenty-four hours. Suddenly a big smile came over her face. She waved us over, welcomed us, and checked us in for the next three weeks.

For the rest of our time there, we met nightly with the new believers, building them up in the Lord and encouraging them in God's ways. We did all we could to prepare for our long-term team to move there three months later. When they did arrive, they found twelve believers who were still meeting faithfully from house to house, continuing to follow Jesus.

It was a great beginning to see a desolate city, once without the gospel, become a beacon of light to that whole province. We were on our way to planting churches.

Have You Ever Seen a Dead Guy?

God continued to move powerfully in Ulan-Ude as believers met together. Our long-term team was established, strengthening new believers and reaching out to the city. After a great visit with the team in the fall of 1992, a group of us stood in a crowded train station in Ulan-Ude, waiting for the train that would take us to a leaders' conference many hours away. It was below freezing, and people were huddled in the station, trying to stay out of the cold.

One of our guys ran up to me and asked, "Have you ever seen a dead guy?"

"I don't think so. Why?"

He pointed and said, "Do you see that guy over there? I think he's dead."

"Are you sure?" I asked.

He looked pale and gray, and about that time he slid out of the chair and bounced on the floor. Some people looked at him but kept walking.

I leaned against the wall, asking God whether we should pray for him to be raised up, send for help, or what. For a moment, I thought, *This might be the moment where we see someone raised from the dead. Surely we should go pray for him.*

While one of our teammates made sure an ambulance was on the way, another teammate and I, along with one of our Russian translators, knelt down next to the man. As I put my hand on his arm, he was cold and clammy. Different phrases began to come to mind from the words of Jesus: *Come forth. Rise up. Be healed.* But none of those phrases seemed to work.

As I opened my eyes after voicing different hopeless prayers, I realized that people were pressing in all around us. Suddenly it hit me. Spontaneously I turned to our translator and said, "Whatever I do, you do."

Then I jumped up and began to cry out, "This man is dead, and some-day you will be too! The question is, do you know Jesus? Have your sins been forgiven? Do you know that He has a place for you in heaven? Everyone will die, and everyone needs to know Jesus. Does anyone here need Jesus?"

Many raised their hands, saying, "I need Jesus!"

I led them in prayer to receive Christ. Then I told them to place their hands on a part of their body that needed healing. We prayed and believed God to touch their bodies and make them whole. People began to scream and testify that God was healing them. The commotion drew an even larger crowd, so I started again: "This man is dead ... "

Even after the man's body was taken away, we continued to preach to the crowd. Hundreds came to faith that day in the station. Our train arrived to take us to our conference several hours away, but I told the members of our team who were not going with us to stay at the train station and pray for people. They remained for another two hours as God moved and many more were saved and healed. And the church continued to grow in Ulan-Ude.

A Vision for the Nations

While some of us were away from Ulan-Ude for a few days, Kevin Johnson, who eventually became the pastor of the church there, stayed behind. He met with one of the home groups and taught them how to hear the Lord. He told them to wait and ask God if there was anything He had to say to them. If God gave them an image, a word, or a Scripture, they should speak it out.

A young girl spoke first. She saw an image of a map with crosses going from Ulan-Ude down to Ulaanbaatar, Mongolia, and then down into China. The crosses also stretched to the right and the left around the globe as far as she could see. She heard the Holy Spirit say, "What has started in Ulan-Ude will spread into Asia and around the whole world." Little did she know that God had been telling us the same thing: Isaiah 54:2–3 was not just for Waco but for our new churches as well.

Establishing the Church

God was fulfilling His promise that "your descendants … will resettle the desolate cities." At one time we believed the Scripture had been fulfilled as the church-planters among us went to Ulan-Ude, but we came to understand that as the church there became an extension of our church body, they should also go forth to inhabit other desolate cities. The church in Ulan-Ude would multiply.

Within the next five years, more than twenty-five people would stay in Ulan-Ude for a year or more as team members, and more than two hundred short-term missionaries would go to do outreach, facilitate sports camps, and lead special seminars to serve the Ulan-Ude community. After five years of raising up Russian leaders and working alongside them, we turned the church completely over to Russian leadership. That church is still flourishing today and reaching people for Jesus in their city and surrounding provinces.

Inheriting a Dream in Irkutsk

Danny and Kathy Mulkey, their two teenagers, and a second church-planting team moved to Russia, this time to the city of Irkutsk in Siberia. A training school team from Waco had been there and shared the gospel with students, seeing many of them come to Jesus and begin to gather in small groups. By the time the long-term team arrived in 1993, the group of students was already meeting regularly on Friday nights.

Over the next couple of years, the church in Irkutsk multiplied their small groups until about a hundred people were gathering on Sunday mornings. They devoted themselves to relationship, discipleship, and community. Modeling what they had learned in Waco, the team saw the church in Irkutsk established. After the Mulkeys returned to the States two years later, Lyle and Melissa Smith emerged as the team leaders, and the church continued to grow and mature.

Alexey Kuschenko was only sixteen years old when he joined the church in Irkutsk, but he quickly matured in his faith. He had come to know Jesus as a high school student during one of our first summer outreaches in Ulan-Ude in 1992, and he had later gone to Irkutsk to attend college. Alexey eventually married a young woman named Margarita, who had been saved through one of the Irkutsk outreaches and was already active in the church when Alexey moved from Ulan-Ude. Both became leaders, disciplers, and evangelists, giving their hearts wholeheartedly to God's work in Irkutsk. When it was time for the church-planting team to return to Waco in 1999, it was obvious that Alexey should take over leadership of the church. Even though he was only twenty-one at the time, God had blessed him with wisdom and steadfastness.

God continued to grow and develop the church in Irkutsk as they learned to love God, love others, and love the lost. In particular, God gave them a heart for those addicted to drugs and people living with HIV/AIDS. Irkutsk has one of the highest rates of HIV infection in Russia, mostly affecting teens and young adults. The church in Irkutsk saw many come to Christ and be set free from addiction as they sought to meet the most extreme needs in their city in the name of Jesus.

Many family members of those in greatest need also came to faith. At one time, Alexey communicated to us that eighty-five percent of the church had been saved out of drug addiction or healed in some way or was a family member of someone who had been saved or healed.

Multiplying the Church

As Alexey and the leaders in Irkutsk were experiencing passion for Jesus and His purposes in their midst, it was spreading to others as well. A young Chinese man, whom we call Larry, came to Irkutsk to study in a language program. He met Christ through some of our team and was discipled in a Lifegroup. Larry eventually became a Lifegroup leader and learned how to invest in others and to reproduce the life of Jesus. After being with the church in Irkutsk for a year and a half, his visa expired, and he had to return to China. Our team prayed for Larry and sent him out, hoping to keep in touch.

Two years passed without any contact from Larry. But Misha, one of the Russian leaders in Irkutsk, and his American wife, Stephanie, had a heart for China. God had given them a desire to go to Larry's city to see a church established there.

When they visited that city, they connected with Larry. While they were visiting over tea, they asked Larry, "Are you still following Jesus?"

Larry looked at them quizzically as if to say, "Well, of course I'm still following Jesus."

"Have you found the underground church or other people to worship with?" they asked.

Larry answered, "All I did when I got here was what you told me to do. I gathered my friends and told them about my faith and what God was doing. Many of them came to Christ, and we began to meet in my home to talk about growing together in Jesus. They began reaching out and starting their own groups. Now we have one hundred and twenty people meeting in different homes in the city."

Misha and Stephanie spent the next two years with Larry and saw the group grow to about seven hundred believers.

The Irkutsk church continues to bear fruit and flourish today. Under Alexey and Margarita's leadership, the believers there continue to reach people in the city, plant churches, and help others find healing for their brokenness in Jesus.

Impossible Dreams in Mongolia

Jackie came to Baylor as a freshman in love with Jesus. She was tender and compassionate and shared Christ boldly. She also struggled with an eating disorder. That bondage led to her dropping out of school after her junior year. After receiving counseling and medical help, she returned to Baylor, still loving Jesus. She and Laura became close friends.

When I was a senior at Baylor, I met a freshman named Bret. He had suffered a sports injury in high school that caused migraine headaches almost daily and chronic, severe pain that was so intense he could hardly focus to study. Doctors had tried everything they could think of, but his neck ligaments had been so damaged that there was nothing they could do. Bret met Jesus in that journey, and by abiding in Him, he found focus and peace, allowing him to study, learn, and function socially.

Bret had been a broken man, hungry for Jesus. He was intent on knowing all there was to know about God. When he and I talked for the first time outside his apartment sitting in his car, the presence of the Lord filled the vehicle. Throughout Bret's college years we met regularly to jog together, to talk about Jesus, and to worship and pray together in the mornings. More and more Bret entered into the power and joy that God had for him.

Jackie and Bret met the weekend of Laura's and my wedding. They discovered they had kindred hearts, both in desiring to live wholeheartedly for Jesus and in a love for the unreached. Eventually they married, believing God had called them to Asia. On their honeymoon, they went to Epcot's World Showcase at Disney World, where they saw a film in the Asian exhibit featuring landmarks of China, as well as the plains of Mongolia. As they watched and heard about Mongolia, which at that time was an isolated country, their hearts were stirred. With tears flowing, they stayed through three showings of the film as people filed in and out around them. They knew God was speaking to them.

Jackie and Bret had been a part of the original team that led college Lifegroups in the early 1990s, learning how to disciple, evangelize, and reproduce the body of Christ. They multiplied their group four different times and were diligent to serve wherever possible in our growing movement. As we labored together, we continued to ask the Lord, "Is now the time for Bret and Jackie to be sent out?" And we continued to wait.

One day as Bret walked out of work, a woman who had been praying for him approached him and asked about Mongolia. When she did, the presence of the Lord touched him so strongly that he was moved to tears. He went home and shared the experience with Jackie, and the presence of the Lord touched her as well. It was time for them to go.

Mongolian Movement

After finishing the training school in 1993, Bret, Jackie, and three single team members left for Ulaanbaatar, Mongolia, to see a church-planting movement established. During the early days they saw fruit from their work, as college students came to Christ and began to meet from house to house. But they found it difficult to develop leaders.

Bret and Jackie began to ask God to raise up a Mongolian leader, someone who would rise up among the people to move them forward. Around that time Jackie developed a relationship with her neighbor, Chuka, a woman who suffered in her home with an alcoholic husband. Through her relationship with Jackie, she heard the gospel and came to Christ. Jackie began teaching Chuka to pray for her husband, Tsolgi, while Bret engaged Tsolgi in conversations about God's wisdom for the family in Scripture and about Jesus. After much prayer and walking through a particularly difficult time of spiritual warfare, Tsolgi eventually gave his heart to Jesus.

As Bret discipled him, Tsolgi shared his faith with his mother. The seventy-year-old woman was a devout Marxist, teaching Marxism at the only medical school in the nation. Every medical student in Mongolia had to take her class. When she heard the message of Jesus and saw how Tsolgi's and Chuka's lives had changed, she also gave her life to Christ. She became as passionate about Jesus as she had been about Marxism. She and Tsolgi led twenty-five adult members of their family to the Lord. That family became the core of multiple home groups all over the city. God did signs and wonders in their midst, and many were saved.

While God was doing great things among them, the new church knew there was more that God had for them. They began to pray for the people in the villages and towns around them who had never heard the gospel. Then they took their first short-term trip to another town in Mongolia. The mayor of that town and about seventy others gave their hearts to the Lord, were baptized, and began meeting from house to house.

Raised from the Dead

In 2006, the Mongolian believers were going to a nearby village of about 12,000 people to reach out to the neighbors and friends of those who had become Christians. During one visit, they heard of a man who was dying of liver cancer, and on their next visit, they learned that the man, who was not a

Christian yet, had died. For thirty-eight hours he'd had no signs of life, so the doctors pronounced him dead and sent his body home for burial. The man's family had gathered and were preparing for his funeral.

One of the Mongolian believers thought God wanted her to go and pray for the dead man. However, the family was Buddhist and would not allow it. They actually thought she was making fun of them. But the man's brokenhearted mother finally relented and allowed the believer to pray for her dead son. The Mongolian believer placed her hand on the dead man and prayed for him to live. His eyelids moved some, but nothing else happened. Eventually she and the other believers left the village and went back to the capital city.

The following week the believers returned to the small village, and the "dead" man was waiting for them alive as he could be! He told them he had certainly been dead, saying, "There was nothing at all." Then when she prayed for him, he suddenly heard her praying and saw a brilliant, bright light. His consciousness returned. He tried to speak to her as she prayed, but he couldn't talk or move at all. After she left the house, his strength slowly returned.

The man asked for something to drink about four hours after the believer's prayer, to the utter shock of his family. Then he got out of bed and started walking around the town, looking for "the Jesus people." When the newly living man found them, he gave his life to Jesus and was baptized. Others came to faith, too. A total of fourteen people were baptized together with him, including his wife, family members, and neighbors—along with the doctor who had pronounced him dead. That man was a forty-seven-year-old taxi driver, well known by the people in the village. Since then, it appears that all 12,000 people in his village have heard about the miracle God performed.

A freshman with an eating disorder and a young man with a physical disability said, "Jesus is enough. He is my portion and my cup. I will not let go of the hem of His garment. I will find my inheritance in Christ alone and give myself to the nations of the earth." They went from being wounded students at Baylor to seeing a church-planting movement established and the dead coming to life.

Today the church in Mongolia continues to move forward as the original vision is still being fulfilled through incredible Mongolian leaders. They have also been planting churches among the Mongol descendants in China and other parts of Asia. In the summer of 2013, under the leadership of Josh and Tsagaanaa Crosslin, the movement also birthed a new initiative to see a church planted among young professionals and college students in Ulaanbaatar so that a new generation of Mongolians would continue to reproduce the glory of God in all the earth. Over the last twenty years, through the ups and downs of life, the original vision continues to move forward through our precious Mongolian friends and leaders.

Church-Planting Growth Pains

Russia, Mongolia, Uzbekistan, Afghanistan—within a few years, we had church planting teams in all of these places and more. To keep up with the rapid growth, we chose to send people out quickly. We soon found it is better to send out the right laborers than to send out an abundance of laborers.

Not everyone we sent out was prepared and mature enough to handle the challenges and complexities of cross-cultural missions. Basically, if someone had faith, wanted to go, and was not in major sin, we sent them. Later on, though, we realized that it takes more than faith for someone to navigate a cross-cultural church plant. We found they needed more training, restoration of their own lives, and consistent pastoral care in order to flourish.

Because of the multitude of laborers we sent out and the pace at which we sent them, we experienced some backlash. A couple of people fell into immorality, and conflict hindered the effectiveness of a few teams. We had to adapt and respond quickly to crises on the field. To say the least, it was a crazy time as we visited teams. It seemed that we were spending the majority our time resolving difficult issues.

In response to all of these challenges, we changed some of our training and leader evaluation processes. One of our new favorite sayings became, "We'd rather deal with it on this side of the water than the other side." Eventually all these things worked together for good as we learned the balance between releasing people quickly and making sure they were equipped to do what God has called them to do.

In 1997, we held a celebration to turn the Ulan-Ude church fully over to Russian leadership. We had been the first foreigners to work in Ulan-Ude, but after 1992, other mission agencies, some of the largest in the world, had come, too. They had better strategies and ideas than we did and had often been critical of our methods.

On the day we turned the church over to the national leaders, several guys from the other organizations came and sat in the back. Joe Ewen, our close friend and mentor from Scotland, was also there. The men asked Joe, "How did these guys do this? We see so many holes in their strategy and missiology."

"You know," Joe said, "sometimes I've wondered the same thing. But one thing I know is that they love Jesus with all their hearts. They fast. They pray. They give their lives sacrificially for people. I guess God just honors that and overlooks their weaknesses."

I love what 2 Corinthians 4:7 says: "We have this treasure in earthen vessels, so that the surpassing greatness of the power will be of God and not from ourselves."

> GOD'S PLAN IS FOR HIS CHURCH TO BE ESTABLISHED AMONG ALL THE PEOPLES OF THE EARTH. THE QUESTION IS NOT WHETHER HE WANTS TO DO IT; THE QUESTION IS WHETHER WE WILL GO.

CHAPTER 11

ANTIOCH BECOMES A CHURCH

And he left for Tarsus to look for Saul; and when he had found him, he brought him to Antioch. And for an entire year they met with the church and taught considerable numbers; and the disciples were first called Christians in Antioch.

ACTS 11:25-26

I was standing on a makeshift stage, in the Heart O' Texas (HOT) exhibit hall in June of 1999. The smell of beer and cigarettes from the party the night before still filled the air. I never would have thought that this would be the starting place of a new era for us – the beginning of Antioch Community Church.

Highland Baptist Church had given us the perfect training ground and a wonderful church family for Laura and me and all of our leaders who were serving locally and around the world. In 1997, we began to dialogue about what it would look like for us to plant our own church. Highland's rich tradition of empowerment and mission was about to become a part of our story as well. In April 1999, Barry Camp, the senior pastor, and Highland's elders, blessed us to plant Antioch Community Church and sent us out to continue to follow the dreams God had put in our hearts.

Antioch Community Church Is Born

For the first several months as a new church plant, we met all around the city of Waco. During the week, Lifegroups gathered in homes and on Sundays we met in a variety of places, from the fairgrounds to the convention center to a local theater. Traveling around to different venues made us a volunteer-driven church. It took more than a hundred volunteers each week to load the trailer, unpack it, set up the venue, take care of the kids, and tear everything down at the end. Those volunteers not only made worship services happen on Sundays, but they also carried the values of who we were and lived them out practically. Even though the process sometimes felt unstable, having to rely so heavily on God and one another forced us to be a people who lived out the things we said we believed.

One particular Sunday, after we had outgrown the HOT, we met at a place called Melody Ranch, a local country-and-western bar. It was a lot of fun, and we felt right at home walking into the smells that came with meeting in a bar. In weeks prior we had used a six-foot horse trough for baptisms. We simply took it with us wherever we met, filled it with water, and baptized people in it. The guy at Melody Ranch graciously offered to let us use the horse trough they used for beer so we wouldn't have to haul ours. What he failed to mention was that his trough was only four feet long—two feet shorter than ours.

Several people were to be baptized that morning at Melody Ranch, including a local anesthesiologist. When he had invited his family to come to see him get baptized, he did not know that we would be meeting at Melody Ranch. His family had not come from an Antioch-style background; they were a more formal bunch. There on the back row in coats and ties and nice dresses, they watched as I stuffed this grown man into a four-foot trough. He was a great sport about it, as he shared boldly what the Lord had done for him.

Somehow, the local newspaper heard about our crazy church and sent a reporter to do a story about us. She was at Melody Ranch the morning of the four-foot horse trough baptisms. It just so happened that we were sharing our vision that morning: we want to be everyday, normal people who live out the simple things of the Kingdom with all our hearts. If we will just do that, we can change the world.

Her article, "Everyday Walk with God," landed on the front page of the paper. She did a great job capturing our heart. For us, it seemed like a prophetic message to our city that expressed our desire to be a simple community that walks every day with Jesus, serving a big God. The irony was that the reporter would eventually join our church and become a part of this great adventure with us.

Since we floated from place to place each week, Lifegroups became even more vital to our church's communication and structure. The Sunday morning gathering place was announced each week through our Lifegroup leaders, so people had to be connected to a small group to find our Sunday morning services. In those first two or three years, more people met in Lifegroups than on Sunday mornings. It was a God-ordained time. We had long desired to see people established in house-to-house ministry. It motivated us to learn how to do an even better job facilitating those small groups. As the groups matured, we saw the church multiply in our city, not through a corporate gathering but through individuals reproducing the life of Jesus in other people through discipleship.

A Place to Plant

Even before we started meeting at different venues around the city, we knew we had a long-term commitment to Waco, and we began to ask God whether we should own or rent a building. As we prayed and sought others' counsel, we became convinced that we were to buy a facility and put down permanent roots in our city. We were led to the inner city because we wanted to do church in such a way that it could be reproduced around the world. We wanted to put ourselves in a multicultural situation at home. We found a building, an old grocery store and cafeteria connected together, along with 36,000 square feet of dirty, rodent-infested warehouse space and a collapsing ceiling. When we inquired about the place, we learned that although it had not been officially inhabited in ten years, prostitutes and drug addicts were living in it at the time. It was the perfect place to start.

We needed $150,000 to purchase the building. We were committed not to go into debt. If we were going to buy something, we would pay cash. But in those days $150,000 seemed like a big mountain to climb. As different groups gathered, we asked everyone to pray and give toward that end. By midnight on the day the money was needed, we had $152,000 to begin the great journey. Once again, God was faithful to provide for all our needs.

Across the street from our newly owned building, a couple of friends working in real estate bought an old house for us to use as office space. The years of chipped paint made the walls multicolored. The cracked windows made for free air-conditioning in the winter, and the rats running through provided ample distraction as we tried to work. It was a great place to start the process of seeing God's work established in and through us.

Renovation Begins

Buying the old grocery store was just the first step in establishing ourselves in Waco. The huge task of renovating lay ahead of us. It wasn't much to look at, dilapidated inside and out, but the structure was strong.

To start work on that old building, we knew it would help to have the architectural drawings so we could see the structural layout. The last company to own the property was the H-E-B Corporation, a grocery store chain in Texas. When we called their records department, we told them we needed the drawings for one of their buildings from 1960, and the man on the phone told us they had shredded everything pre-1990. Then he asked where the building was located, and we told him Waco.

"Oh, you won't believe it," he said, "but I'm from Waco. I thought that particular building was interesting, so I took the drawings and threw them up on the top rack. I think I still have them right here." Talk about a providential phone call.

The church family stepped up to the plate, and volunteers sacrificed a tremendous amount of time and energy to clear it out and get it ready for the renovation. Every once in a while, we conducted a service in the parking lot to encourage everyone through the process. We based our initial fundraising service on the Exodus 35 concept. When it was time to build the tabernacle,

God told the children of Israel to give whatever they had to the cause—jewelry, wood, fabric, or anything else. We asked our people to do the same and give what they had.

We held the first big giving day during a Sunday morning service in the parking lot, and we set out tables to receive anyone's gift. It was amazing to watch. People brought TVs, fur coats, diamond rings, computers, and furniture. You name it, they brought it. Even those without financial resources brought what they had. That morning we collected $294,000 in cash and items that we either used or sold to begin our task of restoring the building debt free.

With the building cleared out and a financial foundation laid, we were ready to get going on the actual work of restoration. A contractor who had been coming to our church told me he wanted to give back in some way.

"Jerry," I said, "what I need is somebody to take the bull by the horns and move this thing forward."

He was just the man to do it. Jerry Dyer and Don Birchum, our foreman, both jumped in feet first and got things moving quickly.

"You just keep pushing forward," I told them, "and I will take care of believing God with our people for the money."

Several times we called the staff together and asked who needed a paycheck that day and who could wait. They anonymously wrote yes or no on a piece of paper so that no one felt guilty and no one came off as a hero. We were just family, doing what was needed. The only people who saw those responses were our administrators, who wrote the checks. I am still blown away by our staff and their willingness to sacrifice what they were rightfully owed.

The Lawn Chair Convention

In July 2000, we realized we were spending $1,500 to $2,000 each week renting space to meet on Sundays. We had already met in the parking lot for motivational services, so we decided to start meeting there every week. The money we saved in rent would go toward the goal of restoring the property debt free.

Sunday morning services in the parking lot were awesome. Because we didn't have money for chairs, we asked people to bring their own. Many carried lawn chairs in the trunks of their cars, and college students showed up each week with couches, recliners, and even park benches. We called it the "Lawn Chair Convention." On a trailer in the back of the crowd, we provided water and sunscreen in the summer and hot chocolate and coffee in the winter. On mornings when it rained, we would pray and ask Jesus to stop the rain for us. I can't tell you how many times the rain dried up just as the service began and then started to fall again as soon as we finished packing up.

One day, however, it started to pour right in the middle of my sermon. I wondered what would happen to the crowd. Some people popped open umbrellas and stayed where they were while others ran under the awning at the front of the building. Everyone stayed through the end of the service. I preached in the rain while being drenched, but the crowd stayed with me all the way. It was amazing to see a people who were so abandoned to Jesus that they would do anything to be in His presence and among His people. That morning, many came to faith.

When I look at Acts 2:42-47, I see a church that met daily in the temple and house to house, breaking their bread together and sharing their lives. This journey for Antioch Community Church was about all of us sharing our lives, sacrificing for one another, and working together to see God's divine purposes realized. We look back on those days with joy and thanksgiving for how God bonded us together as we sacrificed together.

Firm Foundations

It is critical to establish good foundations and impart values in the formative years of a church. When we stepped out in faith into the adventure God had called us to as a church, we began to expand and needed to rally everyone around the common vision and purposes God was laying before us.

We wanted to help people develop from unbeliever to church planter. We would equip, encourage, and nurture along the way so that the lost could be saved and our people could share the gospel consistently. During the first year that we gathered as Antioch Community Church, we taught and reiterated our values so they would be clear.

In our children's ministry we asked the workers to pray for God's purposes and plans over even the smallest child. They developed mission trips for kids and got them involved in engaging the community through evangelism and discipleship. Our youth group embraced our multicultural call by beginning to love and connect with other youth from both the inner city and the suburbs. Our college students became fully integrated into all we were doing and were not just a separate ministry of the church. Our adults took seriously the call to discipleship and commitment. Together, we were becoming a people of common values.

As we looked at staffing the church, we wanted to create an environment of equality. We were a team, and each member mattered, regardless of gifting. We adopted a pattern of paying the same base salary to everyone on our full-time staff, with supplements based on family size. We used the median income of our city as our base income, designed to provide everyone's needs but not necessarily all their wants.

We wanted to make sure that everyone on our staff was called to ministry. Working at Antioch would not be about a job or a paycheck. It would be because of a calling. Whether serving as an administrative assistant or a pastor, everyone is called to the same sacrifice, even when it requires extra time or energy. Although we have adapted our model through the years to consider years of service and differing responsibilities, the heart and the principles have remained the same.

From the very beginning, at least twenty percent of our church budget has been set aside for missions through our church. We have also set aside five to ten percent of the money raised for our building projects to bless other churches and ministries. I've seen God abundantly bless us as we have given away hundreds of thousands of dollars to other like-hearted and like-minded churches and ministries, both in our city and around the world. God is not asking us to just take care of ourselves but to be a vessel to bless others.

One unique opportunity came up a few years ago when a cell phone provider came to us and asked to use part of our parking lot to build a cell tower. As we prayed about it, we felt that God pointed us to His instructions to His people in Leviticus 23:22 to leave the corners of the field for the poor. So a cell tower sat on one corner of our parking lot for the first ten years of the church. The monthly income from the lease went toward feeding the homeless and others in need.

Another one of our early foundations was prayer. We continued to establish five-day-a-week prayer on the campus and to plan multiple other prayer meetings through the week for the church at large. Just as we had done before, we hosted neighborhood parties to love the people in the inner city around us. The Antioch training schools continued to disciple people and to raise up church planters. Antioch Ministries International, our training and sending arm, continued to send out long term workers to the nations.

Abundant Provision

By December 15, 2000, we were in our renovated building. A grocery store had become a sanctuary and home to Antioch Community Church. Not everything was completely finished, but we were able to meet inside. Things had been moving along, and God had provided abundantly for us to get to that point. We had honored all of our commitments to our builders, and we did it all debt free. Our people had sacrificed greatly over the past year.

A few weeks later in January, as we prepared for our Sunday service, we realized we needed $150,000 by the following Monday to pay the next round of bills. From day one, we had said God would be our provision. We wouldn't pressure people to give. If He was leading us to do something, He would provide.

When Sunday came around, I told the church it was time for a family meeting. I read 2 Corinthians 9:6-8: "Now this I say, he who sows sparingly will also reap sparingly, and he who sows bountifully will also reap bountifully. Each one must do just as he has purposed in his heart, not grudgingly or under compulsion, for God loves a cheerful giver. And God is able to make all grace abound to you, so that always having all sufficiency in everything, you may have an abundance for every good deed."

Then I said, "This building will be finished out of cheerful giving, not coercion. We just want to tell you where we are. We need $150,000 by noon tomorrow. We don't know what to do except to lie on our faces before God between now and Monday morning."

That morning, $70,000 came in. A businessman ran up to me and said, "Hey, I know where we can get a loan for the other $80,000. Let me go get it."

"No," I replied. "We have all said that God is our provision. We will live and die off what He has spoken to us. Let's hang in there."

The elders were slated to meet at noon on Monday to assess the situation. All morning people were calling and coming by to give what they had. One guy had recently opened a savings account with $1,000, and he gave it all. Kids brought in piggy banks and emptied them before us. One family was saving up for a much-needed second vehicle, and they gave their entire savings. Young and old alike brought in change and possessions, everything they had.

When we met at noon, our accountant tallied up all that had been brought in and reported that we had made it. We had $153,000!

We whooped and hollered, celebrating God's amazing provision. Just as we were about to go tell everybody the good news, I got a phone call. The person on the other end was contacting us on behalf of a foundation in a large city in Texas. A donor had told them to call us at noon on the dot to tell us that someone was anonymously donating $100,000. No one knew it at the time, but I had been secretly praying, asking God to provide a gift of $100,000 for us. I had heard of such things happening for other organizations, so I asked God to bring such a miracle to us as well. And He did. After our people had given everything they had to get us to the amount we needed, God gave us $100,000 more.

I got so excited that I ran over to the building where people—many of them unbelievers—were working, and I told them to stop their work and gather together. "I just wanted to tell you all what God has done for us!" I exclaimed. I told them about God's miraculous provision and then shouted, "And you're gonna get paid!" Believer and unbeliever alike saw the evidence of God's faithfulness to His people.

The extra $100,000 gave us a boost to continue on our journey of faith. But we still had plenty of opportunities to continue to trust God along the way. With just a few parts of the building left to finish, we got a phone call that we needed $12,000 by 5:00 the next afternoon to pay a vendor. The vendor happened to be one of our dear friends who had given us hundreds of volunteer hours. His company needed the money we owed him, and we were determined to give it to them.

The next day, I gathered the elders and said, "If this doesn't come in by the afternoon, I'm going to sell my truck at the local dealership." After praying together we felt we were supposed to wait and watch God work. About noon I locked my office door and got on my face before God, determined to stay there until He provided. The phone rang at 2:00 p.m. It was the front desk receptionist. "Someone dropped off a check," she said. "You might want to come see it."

The check was for $13,000. A young man had brought the tithe from his signing bonus with a major league baseball team. He had been a student at Baylor, and since we were his church, he felt compelled that particular day not to wait until Sunday but to bring in his tithe that same day. I love how God works, causing us to depend on Him wholeheartedly so He can glorify Himself in the end.

The building was complete in April 2001. Finally, after almost two years of giving, sacrificing, working, praying, and trusting God for every penny, the Antioch community was able to rejoice together in the $1.5 million building project completed without the burden of debt. God stretched our faith to the limits, but through it we grew together as a family during that season.

In April, after the building was completed, I was sitting on my couch spending time with the Lord. I asked Him, "What's next for us as a church?" As I was praying a picture came to my mind of the belly of our building bowing out, bursting at the seams with a hundred different rivers flowing over the horizon. It seemed that God was saying that if we will simply love, honor, and obey Him in this place, then people will be sent out to our city, this nation, and the nations of the earth. *Wow*, I thought, *Lord, let it be.*

> GOD BUILDS HIS CHURCH THROUGH THE SACRIFICE AND PARTNERSHIP OF HIS PEOPLE. THE GREAT ADVENTURE IS ALWAYS BASED ON A PEOPLE LIVING BEYOND THE COMFORTABLE AND DEPENDING ON THE MIRACULOUS.

CHAPTER 12

FROM PRISON TO PRAISE

So Peter was kept in the prison, but prayer for him was
being made fervently by the church to God.

ACTS 12:5

"We came here to give our lives for the Afghan people, not to save our lives. Whatever happens is okay because Jesus is worthy of our lives."

Once again I was in awe of the men and women on our Afghan team as I stood in their living room in Kabul, Afghanistan, in June of 2001. Little did I realize that their statements of faith would almost become a reality.

On August 3, 2001, I got a call from Dawn, the administrator of our international work. Dayna Curry and Heather Mercer, two of our Afghan team members, had been arrested by the Taliban secret police for showing *The Jesus Film* to an Afghan family.

Our teams had been working in repressive countries like Afghanistan for several years, so we'd faced challenges before. We assumed with a bit of negotiation we could get them released quickly, but this was different. The Taliban had been threatening foreign aid workers in Afghanistan for months, and they had recently sent out a decree to the foreign community declaring that proselytizing by non-Muslims would mean a minimum of fourteen days of imprisonment. If there had been conversions, they could face the death penalty.

For four years we had a team that worked and lived under the Taliban regime. The team leader and his family lived in a home with a Taliban commander on one side and a mullah, who was an Islamic spiritual leader, on the other. Over time they had developed a good relationship with both of these men's families. The team had successfully navigated difficult circumstances as they ministered to Afghans through education and health care. As always they were sharing both their lives and the message of the gospel to those who were open.

Coming Together

When I received Dawn's phone call, I was twelve hours from home. Laura and I had taken the kids on a vacation after the Antioch family had officially paid the last bill for the completion of our building. So many things raced through my mind. The first was to call our people to prayer. I didn't want to cause a huge alarm, though, so I asked Dawn to gather our Lifegroup leaders and to begin to pray around the clock for Dayna, Heather, and the six other aid workers who had been imprisoned. I got back into town at midnight and went straight to the church with my sleeping bag in hand, thinking we might be there two or three days praying for the girls' release. When I arrived, the prayer room was already full, and people were scheduled hourly to pray over the next few days. After the previous two years of trusting together through our building journey, our people knew how to rally in prayer.

During the first few days of Dayna and Heather's imprisonment, we tried to keep it out of the press. The State Department was working with the Taliban to negotiate their freedom, and we didn't want to complicate matters by connecting them with our church. As the details began to unfold, though, we realized this had not just been a random arrest. Not only were the secret police involved, but we later learned that Mohammed Omar, the leader of the Taliban, was also involved in the decisions regarding their continued imprisonment. This made the situation far more serious than we first believed. We realized that simple negotiation would not be enough to see them released.

On the morning of August 4, we met together as an elder team to ask God for His wisdom. As we talked, prayed, and looked at the Scriptures, we realized there were three possible outcomes seen in the Bible. First, people were imprisoned for long periods of time and wrote great letters from their jail cells that have helped people for hundreds of years. Second, people were imprisoned and eventually died for their faith. The most honorable deaths in Scripture belong to those who gave their lives for what they believed in just as their Lord did. And third, there were those imprisoned who, through the miraculous intervention of God, were released and able to testify to the goodness of God in the midst of their imprisonment. All three of these scenarios brought glory to God, but we believed that God had chosen scenario number three for Dayna and Heather. We prayed out of Acts 12:5-17:

"So Peter was kept in the prison, but prayer for him was being made fervently by the church to God. On the very night when Herod was about to bring him forward, Peter was sleeping between two soldiers, bound with two chains, and guards in front of the door were watching over the prison. And behold, an angel of the Lord suddenly appeared ... saying, 'Get up quickly.' And his chains fell off his hands. And the angel said to him ... 'Wrap your cloak around you and follow me.' ... When they had passed the first and second guard, they came to the iron gate that leads into the city, which opened for them by itself; and they went out and went along one street, and immediately the angel departed from him. ... He went to the house of Mary ... where many were gathered together and were praying. ... Peter continued knocking; and when they had opened the door, they saw him and were amazed. But motioning to them with his hand to be silent, he described to them how the Lord had led him out of the prison."

We clung to this passage over the three and a half months Dayna and Heather were in prison. When doubt crept in, we prayed more fervently, believing God would deliver them and the other aid workers.

A few Antioch staff members and I went to Pakistan several times over those hundred-plus days to meet with the U.S. State Department representatives and lawyers involved in the case, as well as to care for our other Afghan team members who had escaped the Taliban's raid. Danny Mulkey, our international director at that time, spent ten weeks in Pakistan gathering information and working with whomever necessary to see the girls released.

When the tragedy of 9/11 occurred, a little over a month after Dayna and Heather's capture, we knew they, along with the other foreign workers who had been arrested at the same time would feel immediate ramifications. This was now an international incident with political consequences. As we grieved with the rest of the country over the losses of 9/11, we also braced ourselves for what would lie ahead.

Until that point, press coverage on Dayna and Heather's imprisonment had been limited, but after 9/11, it became national news. We decided to use the coverage as an opportunity to ask other believers to join with us in prayer. We held a press conference with reporters from several national papers and the Associated Press to answer questions the media had been asking. Our prayer was that they would pick up the story in its purest form so we could effectively call people to pray for Dayna, Heather, the other prisoners, and the nation of Afghanistan. Miraculously, that is exactly what happened.

One key writer worked for the *Austin American-Statesmen*. He was not a believer, but he was drawn to the story. After sitting down with me to get the details straight, he wrote an article that clearly represented our hearts in the matter. His full-page story was picked up by the *Drudge Report*, which communicated the story to millions of readers. Suddenly, we were not the only ones called to pray, but people all over the country also heard the story and began to intercede with us.

Over the next three and a half months, the people who interceded in our prayer room were deeply affected. Even as we were going through the greatest challenge of our lives, renewal was happening in our midst. Whenever we pray and give ourselves to God's causes, He changes us.

Greater New Light Baptist Church, an African-American church nearby, felt led by the Lord to pray for Dayna and Heather one Sunday evening. They stayed up all night praying for their release. A group of Antioch men were in the prayer room on a Monday morning for their weekly 5:00 a.m. prayer time when the Greater New Light group knocked at the door. The two groups joined together in seeking God's deliverance for Dayna and Heather.

We received letters from around the country. We believe that millions were interceding for the prisoners in Kabul. The body of Christ in Waco and around the world was unified in praying for their release.

Dayna, Heather, and the six other foreigners believe God allowed them to be captured in order to awaken the world to His heart for Afghanistan. I believe that, too. The Taliban, a regime that did not believe in freedom for men, women, or children, were oppressing widows, orphans, and others who were vulnerable. God allowed some of His children to be put in prison so the cry of the orphan and widow could be heard and the prayers of God's people could break the back of that oppressive regime. I don't believe God was only interested in the release of two young Americans—I believe He was interested in freedom for an entire nation.

Worldwide Media

Perhaps one of the most unique opportunities that surfaced during this season came through our daily interaction with national and international reporters. Overnight, we went from being an unknown church to being inundated with requests for interviews. As requests poured in to meet with us, we asked God for wisdom to know which ones to accept and which ones to turn down. We knew media coverage could either be a blessing or a curse, and our desire was never to become celebrities. So, wanting to be solely led by the Holy Spirit in our decisions, sometimes we declined requests from prominent news agencies and talk shows, and other times we accepted.

As we met with so many interviewers during those few months, we also took the opportunity to minister to them. We wanted to love and encourage them, while not being intimidated or impressed by them. Their words could either crucify us or make us heroes, and we had no control over which they chose. We trusted God to protect us and give us wisdom.

I remember a group from one of the largest news agencies in the world who came to spend a couple of days with us. They visited our service as part of their process. After filming that Sunday, tears filled the main reporter's eyes as he asked me, "What was that presence? I've seen a lot of religious services, but there was something different here. What was it?"

"That's Jesus—the One who loves you and cares for you and died for you," I responded.

As I met with the group the next day, another member of the crew began to ask questions about the reality of Jesus. Before it all ended, these three men, who are well known in media circles, were asking for prayer and more insight into the life of Christ.

During this season, several questions came up both in conversations and interviews about our beliefs and values. One common one was, "Do you believe that Christians are the only ones going to heaven and that Muslims are going to hell?" I would always ask the Lord for wisdom in answering questions like these. My response was, "In John 14:6, Jesus said, 'I am the way, and the truth, and the life; no one comes to the Father but through Me.'" Whether someone calls himself or herself Christian, Muslim, Hindu, or Buddhist, these words are still true. It is not the label that we call ourselves, but the God we choose that determines our eternal destiny. If it were my opinion, that would be one thing, but this is what Jesus said about Himself, and I have chosen to follow Him."

Another question that came up was, "Is it right to offer aid and also share your faith? Don't people feel obligated to respond to your message if you are helping them practically?" My response to this was to explain that when I look at the life of Jesus' followers, they were always doing both: boldly proclaiming Christ as the way to eternal life *and* sacrificially giving everything they had to serve the poor and needy.

Sometimes I would tell reporters, "We want to be Billy Graham and Mother Teresa combined. We want to be clear with our message of salvation in the same way Billy Graham has been through the years, and we want to serve the poor as Mother Teresa did. No matter how people respond, it is still right to care for their needs."

During a radio program interview with Dayna, Heather, and me after their release, a well-known pastor asked me if I felt responsible or guilty for their imprisonment in Afghanistan. He asked me, "How did you deal with the question of what might happen to their lives?"

I explained to him our journey. "When I was with them in Afghanistan in June, we knew the risks of living out our faith wholeheartedly in an oppressive Muslim regime. We knew that people had gone before us and sacrificed their very lives for what they believed in. I cried many tears on behalf of Dayna and Heather, longing for their release. But we all realized that this mission we are a part of may one day cost us our lives. They had already decided that Jesus is worthy, and their lives were not their own."

To God Be the Glory

On November 14, 2001, the worldwide press descended on Waco. Russian President Vladimir Putin was meeting with President George W. Bush at his ranch in Crawford, which is only twenty minutes from our church. National media as well as international reporters from Russia and several European countries were in town to cover this story. That morning, since the press was in town, they asked us to hold a press conference to give an update on the situation in Afghanistan.

Throughout the entire time Dayna and Heather had been in prison, we received many false rumors about their release. We had learned not to get too excited until we could verify whatever news we heard. During the press conference that morning, one reporter told us that the Taliban had fled Kabul with Dayna and Heather. We had heard that rumor, too, but couldn't validate it, so we dismissed it and went on with the press conference.

That day went on as most days: we prayed and continued taking care of the needs of the church. Then, at 5:15 p.m., a man from CBS burst through the front door of our offices with a big camera screaming, "I want an interview now! What is your response?"

"My response to what?" I asked.

"The girls were released from prison. All the foreigners have been found and are being flown to Pakistan right now. Lock the doors—I get the exclusive!"

"Who did you get that information from?" I asked.

We ran to a television and turned on the *CBS Evening News* with Dan Rather. He was reporting exactly what the man had said, showing a Pakistani helicopter landing in Islamabad. Spontaneous joy broke out in the office.

In the midst of the chaotic rejoicing, we did not lock down the doors. Other news crews came streaming in the front door. I told them we would make a statement at 6:15 p.m. in our auditorium. One of our pastors called the Life-group leaders with the news and invited everyone to the church to celebrate. People started flowing in until hundreds were gathered in the auditorium. Everyone was rejoicing. Our people had owned this in their hearts and were seeing with their own eyes the very things they had prayed for.

Our worship leader, James Mark Gulley, was there, and I asked him to lead a time of worship after the statement. As he warmed up, it was so inspiring that I told him to just go for it right then and there. News crew members were setting up microphones for my statement when James Mark started singing and our people joined in with tears, raised hands, and much joy. As we all began to dance and sing, the press went crazy. They were running around with cameras, taking photos, and getting video.

Then I started thinking, *You know, for the last three months, the press has never really let me share my whole heart. When I talked about Jesus, they edited it out. Now, I am about to go live across the world with an unedited version of our story. This is an incredible opportunity—I get to preach the gospel.*

When we finished the song, I approached the microphones and began our live statement. I shared Dayna's story, Heather's story, and my story and thanked God for His delivering hand. Then I ended by saying, "We love the Lord Jesus. We are thankful for His faithfulness. We are thankful He offers that love to all people. Whoever calls on His name can be saved from all the junk that goes on inside of us. We can be free because of what He has done. We see people like Dayna and Heather, who are willing to lay their whole lives down for that precious good news that Jesus is Lord. We are so proud of these ladies, who they are, and what they stand for. And we are thankful most of all to the God who makes a way where there is no way."

I still remember one news agency in Dallas that had shown the live feed from our auditorium. When the camera went back to the anchors, they looked frozen for a couple of seconds before one of them awkwardly stammered, "Oh, well, they are really excited in Waco, Texas."

That night we worshipped and prayed for three more hours, doing interviews with the press, sharing the gospel, and proclaiming the goodness of God. For the next twenty-four hours, the lead for the BBC radio news brief went something like this: "Jesus loves Afghanistan from Waco, Texas! They are celebrating at the church of Dayna Curry and Heather Mercer, two aid workers who had been released from imprisonment in Afghanistan." In the background, you could hear a song that James Mark had written during their imprisonment called "Jesus Loves Afghanistan." The next day, photos of our people dancing and rejoicing were plastered on the front pages of many newspapers across the United States.

It was an incredible night of celebration for all of us. For Dayna, Heather, and the six other aid workers, it was a victory. For the body of Christ, it was a victory. Eventually, for the orphans and widows of Afghanistan, it would be a victory. Dayna and Heather were able to endure prison and go on to serve Jesus in other places because they lived out the simple values of the Kingdom.

Dayna's and Heather's lifestyles became public, but there are hundreds of others in our midst who live the same way, out of a love for Jesus, a love for others, and a love for the lost. When you have an everyday walk with God, whether the whole world knows it or nobody knows it, it will change the world.

An Enduring Testimony

On November 16, 2001, when I met Dayna and Heather in Pakistan, I told them they were about to enter an incredible world of people wanting to exploit their story. I told them they had to decide: do you want to be like Mother Teresa or like a Christian rock star?

They immediately responded, "We got in this for the poor and the lost. How do we stay true to that?"

"First of all," I advised, "you have got to decide what to do with the money you will make from telling your story." They didn't realize that the American press had made them famous and their story would have great value.

They decided to set up a charity to give the proceeds of speaking engagements, interviews, and books to help the people of Afghanistan, pouring back into the lives of those they went to see set free. No matter where the journey took Dayna and Heather, from national television shows to writing their book, *Prisoners of Hope,* they were not motivated by money. They simply wanted to point to the goodness of the Lord.

Our annual retreat for Antioch missionaries from around the world was slated to begin in Germany on November 17. I flew from Pakistan with Dayna and Heather, and we were able to be at the opening session together with our people. As these young ladies shared their story with their friends and co-laborers from around the world, it stirred all of us to believe that God could meet us in the challenges of working in some of the most difficult countries in the world. He could even meet us in the challenges of being imprisoned for our faith. Their testimony wasn't something that caused us to pull back but to rise up and believe God for even greater things.

> GOD STILL OPENS PRISON DOORS TODAY WHEN
> PEOPLE PRAY. WHETHER IN A PRISON IN AFGHANISTAN
> OR A PRISON OF OUR OWN BROKEN LIVES,
> GOD IS ABLE TO SET THE CAPTIVES FREE.

CHAPTER 13

INTENTIONAL CHURCH

These words, which I am commanding you today, shall be on your heart.
You shall teach them diligently to your sons and shall talk of them
when you sit in your house and when you walk by the way and
when you lie down and when you rise up.

DEUTERONOMY 6:6-7

"What now?"

For months, my focus had been on what was going on in Afghanistan, but after getting Dayna and Heather on a plane back to the States, I was able to think about the future of our church. I began to seek God about what was next.

The answer was so clear that I knew the words were from God: *I want you to bring everybody back to the basics. It's about loving Me, loving others, and loving the lost. This is not to be the "Dayna and Heather church" or the "missions church." Be the church that loves Me, loves others, and loves the lost.*

Our heart at Antioch Community Church was for everyone to be living out the gospel. It wasn't just for college students, and it wasn't just for vocational missionaries. It wasn't just for the few. From the youngest to the oldest, we were all to be followers and disciples of Jesus. This good news was supposed to be lived out—truly lived out—by everyone in our midst.

I realized that my job, and the job of our pastoral team, was to see this come to pass. Ephesians 4:11–12 says, "And He gave some as apostles, and some as prophets, and some as evangelists, and some as pastors and teachers, for the equipping of the saints for the work of service, to the building up of the body of Christ." I looked at it this way: I know I'm doing the work God has called me to do by the number of people in our congregation who are actually living out the gospel. In other words, I am doing my job as a pastor if other people are doing the work of the ministry.

The thing that changes a person's life and makes a church come alive is not agreeing with basic values—it's living them. In order to help people live them, we had to articulate them.

Antioch had eleven values written down at the time. They were all great, all biblical. One day I started off a staff meeting by saying, "Tell me what our eleven values are." No one could remember all eleven. I couldn't even remember all of them myself! So we cut them down to eight.

At the next meeting, one other person and I were the only ones who remembered all eight. So we whittled the list down to five. I told everyone to go home and memorize them. But at the next meeting, only half the people were able to remember all five values.

So we got down to the bare essentials and cut the list to three: Love God. Love others. Love the lost.

Here's the thing: if we wanted to live out church in a way that it could be easily reproduced, then it had to be simple. Somehow, when we nailed down three values, the group not only felt they could remember them, but they felt they could actually do them. Obviously, trying to reproduce a model is more complicated than simply writing down these values, but at least we believed it was possible. So we began to talk about, teach, and model the three values with every person at Antioch, from the youngest to the oldest.

Loving God

We teach that "loving God" means everyone in our church should have a life-giving, meaningful connection with God—meeting with Him day by day in Word, worship, and prayer. And that always begins at home.

When Laura and I had children, we asked each other, "What is the main thing we want our kids to have when they leave our house?" The answer was a devotional life: intentionally meeting every day with Jesus so that whatever happens to them, whatever comes in their lives, they will have learned to connect with God personally. So we trained our kids thoroughly and diligently. When they were as young as two years old, they would sit by us as we read the Bible to them and prayed with them. We bought them a big-letter Bible, and we taught them how to read and then how to pray and then how to journal. Side by side we journeyed with them, and as we did we found that they began to hear God, understand the Bible, and know where to go for the answers in life.

It wasn't enough to focus only on our own children, though, so we began to teach all the kids in the church to spend time with Jesus. Our children's pastor created God Time cards. There were seven cards each week on flip rings, each with a Scripture passage or verse, a prayer, and a place to write something. A beautiful thing happened when the kids took them home: the children began leading. They would go home and say to their parents, "I need to do my God Time cards," and their parents would realize they weren't doing their own God time. Parents would sit with their children to do God time together. Then the parents would start to make time for their own devotional lives.

I began to meet with a group of men who admitted they had known the Lord for years but had never been consistent in their devotional lives. I had observed through the years that the way to help someone with his or her devotional life is not by simply handing out information. Instead, I had these men start meeting me at my office at 5:00 am. I would pray out loud, and then we would read the Bible out loud, listen to worship music together, and journal next to each other. By the fourth day they were able to go through the process on their own because I had modeled each step. To this day, those men would say their devotional life has been their greatest source of strength for their families and their work. That simple process of *showing* people how to do something instead of *telling* them how has changed our congregation from the inside out.

We also encouraged each of our leaders to spend at least thirty minutes a day in worship, prayer, and Bible study. Now, many people might say, "Hey, that's legalism" or, "I can't believe you're actually putting a number on it." But there's a difference between creating a discipline and legalism. It's not legalism if you actually want to do it. If you actually want to have a devotional life with Jesus, and somebody helps you with a few tools, then that's a joy. And honestly we did not want any leaders who weren't spending time with Jesus themselves. People need Jesus moving through the lives of their leaders.

Bottom line, we want loving God to be the central value of our church. Of course, that kind of love is holistic and touches every area of our life, but loving God with all our hearts, minds, souls, and strength begins with our devotional lives.

Loving Others

Loving others can look a thousand different ways, but we established two practical areas related to this truth. We wanted everybody to be part of a Lifegroup, and we wanted everybody to be discipled and then to disciple somebody else. We broke it down like this: community is where you find accountability, friendship, healing, and restoration. Out of that you reach out to others who need the same.

Carrie moved to Waco from West Texas following a disheartening marriage that she went to great lengths to try to hold together. Her ex-husband didn't want to put in the effort to clean up his impurity and salvage their marriage. Despite Carrie's perseverance, their relationship ended in divorce, leaving Carrie as a single mom with their three precious little boys. Carrie had visited our annual missions conference, World Mandate, in a prior year and decided to step out in faith hoping to find a new community at Antioch who would love her and her three boys. With a job that could transfer with her to Waco, she and the boys moved in 2002.

Connie, one of our Lifegroup leaders, met Carrie through a mutual friend and initiated getting to know her. Carrie soon visited the Lifegroup that Connie led with her husband, Shawn. The Lifegroup focused on getting in God's presence together and becoming true community with one another.

While the women in the Lifegroup were intentionally investing in Carrie for her personal growth and restoration, the men in the Lifegroup were stepping in to love the three boys. Although Carrie was a strong, stable woman who cared for her boys tremendously well, there were still some gaps that only a man could fill in the lives of her boys. And because the boys' father lived many hours away, the men of the Lifegroup made a special effort to help them feel valued. The dads made sure they were present for each of the boys' birthday parties, oftentimes going to great lengths to make them special. Couples in the Lifegroup even watched the three boys when Carrie had to go out of town for work.

Carrie's Lifegroup also helped her fulfill a dream she had to take the boys on a mission trip. In 2003, the four of them joined our family mission trip to Juarez, Mexico. Together, she and her boys laid aside their own needs and ministered to others who needed to hear of the saving grace of Jesus Christ. And the Lifegroup was right there, too, helping Carrie with the boys while they learned to minister together.

Ultimately, Carrie wasn't a project. She was a friend, and she and her energetic boys became family. And together, the Lifegroup experienced true community.

That kind of community also included intentional discipleship. In 2 Timothy 2:2, Paul writes, "The things which you have heard from me in the presence of many witnesses, entrust these to faithful men who will be able to teach others also." In addition to attending corporate gatherings and Lifegroups, men were meeting with men and women were meeting with women for intentional discipleship.

We shaped discipleship meetings around the 3 Big Questions that we explained in chapter 7: How is your devotional life and how can I help you? Is there any sin in your life that you need to confess? Who are you reaching out to and how can I help you do that better? According to the 2 Timothy passage, we expect those we disciple to do the same with someone else.

I have heard men say, "I've been in church for years, and I have never been discipled before. Nobody has ever invested in me. No one has ever held me accountable. I'm a good man. I've taught Sunday school, and I've tried to be everything I was supposed to be, but this is changing my life." Many men and women have found power for the first time in their lives to live free from sin, walk in community with others, and become effective in sharing their faith with those around them.

When we talk about "loving others," it needs to be intentional, practical, and reproducible. God never gives us truths just to think about. He gives us truths to follow because it's in our best interest and it's how the world is changed.

Loving the Lost

We also asked our church members to consistently pray for one to three people in their lives who did not know Jesus. Then we taught them how to invite those they'd been praying for into a conversation about Jesus. At that point, they were confident in being able to share the gospel and their personal story of coming to faith in Christ with their friends. And when they did this, stories began to flood in.

Beth, a home-schooling mother of four, found it challenging to get out and share the truth and love of Jesus with others. So she decided to be more proactive with the people she did encounter regularly—those who delivered packages, dropped off the daily mail, or picked up the garbage in her neighborhood. She and her children would set out cold drinks and greet anyone who came by their house. They slowly developed a relationship with Ladi, the UPS driver who delivered packages in their neighborhood.

Even though Ladi didn't stop at their house every day, they could hear his truck and would take drinks outside when he drove by or stopped at a nearby house. After establishing a friendship, Beth asked Ladi, who was originally from Nigeria, if he went to church. He told her that his wife went to church, but that he preferred to watch football. Beth began to share about Antioch and how she experienced God's presence there. For a long time Ladi didn't realize his need for God, but Beth and the kids continued to give him sodas and ask him how he was doing. Over time, God began working in his life.

Ladi and his wife divorced, and he was at an all-time low. He drove by Beth's house on the day his divorce was final. Beth encouraged him and told him that God would help him through this difficult time. She and her kids prayed for him and invited him to church again. More than a year after meeting Beth and the kids, Ladi visited Antioch. He says he felt as though the preacher was talking directly to him. A couple of months later he went to their Lifegroup, where again he experienced the love of Jesus. Beth's husband, Matt, discipled and mentored Ladi, and eventually, he gave his life to Jesus.

The people at his workplace noticed a difference in Ladi's life, and he gave all the glory to God. It was obvious that Ladi was a changed man. He and his wife also reconciled, and she gave her life to Jesus. Their kids gave their lives to Jesus, too. They were baptized in our church and served alongside us for ten years until God moved them to another city. It's those simple initiations of love and prayer that open a window to transformation.

Personally, Laura and I used our children's activities as an opportunity for outreach. As I coached soccer teams, Laura and I would pray intentionally, "Lord, would you give us open doors with the children on the team and their parents?" I purposefully did not tell them I was a pastor because I didn't want that to create distance between us. I wanted just to be one of them and look for open doors along the way.

One year there was a boy on our team whose father struggled with anger. Rick would go into a rage when things didn't go his way, and he had been kicked off the field during games twice that year. He was an easy target for prayer, and we had been praying for him. Later in that season, he saw me on television giving an interview about something our church was involved in with the city. Rick walked up to me at practice the next day and said, "You blankety-blank, you didn't tell me you were a pastor!"

"Oh, well, I didn't want to create any barriers between us," I said.

"I told you dirty jokes! You've seen me fly off the handle. And you didn't tell me you were a pastor?"

"I was waiting for the day we could have a good conversation about it. You ready?"

Rick said, "I've got to get rid of this anger. How are you going to help me?"

So I invited him to meet at my office the next day, and he poured out his life—brokenness, challenges in his second marriage, and struggles with his kids. As we talked, I said, "You know, anger is just a symptom of what's going on inside of you."

As we went a little deeper, Rick said he had always seen God as "the man upstairs," but God had never been real to him. He didn't really understand the gospel or his need for Jesus.

That day, in my office, Rick gave his life to Jesus. Eventually, his wife Terry did the same. Today, Rick and Terry are solid members of Antioch, right in the middle of everything we do. God has touched their personal lives, their marriage and their family. And, through their Lifegroup, they have gained community and friends for a lifetime.

Heartfelt Worship

In building a healthy church around these three values, we can never underestimate the power of coming together week by week in corporate worship. Our Sunday gatherings are an expression of what God is doing in our lives throughout the week. It's a church family coming together to exalt the name of Jesus and express our passion for Him. It's both celebration and fuel for the coming week as people continue to live out the values of loving God, loving others, and loving the lost.

The three key expressions in our Sunday gatherings are heartfelt worship, teaching from the Word of God, and opportunity for prayer and response. Of course, the people who lead you into passionate worship are critical to the values of passion and purpose being modeled correctly to the congregation. We made it clear from the beginning that unless people were living out the values in their own lives, we didn't want them leading from the front. James Mark Gulley came to us in the early days, having fully embraced humility, brokenness, and discipleship out of his great love for Jesus. From the start of the church in 1999, he has sacrificially led us into the presence of God. For me as a leader, James Mark has been a God-ordained partner in ministry, but more than that, he has been a brother and a friend who lives out the values of the Kingdom.

James Mark, his wife, Maria, and the rest of the band members on stage have been invested fully in the vision of the church. They are not on stage for a performance. They worship from the heart. Since the beginning of the church, it has been a requirement for the band members to be actively involved in a Lifegroup, living out their walk with God in community with others. I am so thankful that the Gulleys and the rest of the band live out the values of the Kingdom; it makes their song writing and worship leading authentic and powerful. James Mark has written songs that have carried our hearts through trials and tribulation and expressed the joy and celebration of God in our victories.

God's presence in worship truly contains the power to save people and see them set free. Often, people will comment that simply walking into the auditorium at Antioch has caused them to experience the presence of God powerfully. Before coming to our church, Donna battled drug and alcohol addiction for twenty-five years. After two failed marriages and two near death experiences, Donna met a believer at work who directed her to Antioch. She recalls that she was plagued with demons in her life, ones she could not get rid of. When she walked through the doors at Antioch on a Sunday morning, she felt the familiar sense of chains dragging her down as she had whenever she considered attending other spiritual events. But when she stepped into our auditorium, the worship overwhelmed her. She immediately felt those chains break off, and she gave her life to Jesus that day. Since that day in 2000, Donna has been walking in freedom with Jesus and can be found on the front row worshiping enthusiastically every Sunday.

For all of us at Antioch, that kind of heartfelt worship sends us out the doors each week to continue living out the values of loving God, loving others, and loving the lost.

Survey Says

After four years of living out the three values and reinforcing them through the church, we decided to do a survey to ask, "Is it working? Are these values getting in deep?" We did an anonymous survey, and about a thousand people completed it. The number one question was, "What are the values of the church?" The results showed that 96 percent of our people could say it verbatim: *Love God, love others, and love the lost.* When asked, "What is the motto of the church?" 96 percent got that, too: *A passion for Jesus and His purposes in the earth.* We asked, "Are you spending time with Jesus on a daily basis, three to five times a week, two times or less, or none at all?" We quantified that with "thirty minutes or more." The survey revealed that 62 percent of our people were spending daily time with Jesus thirty minutes or more. Another 28 percent were spending time with Jesus three to five times a week; 8 percent spent two times or less; and only 2 percent were not spending time with Jesus at all. An amazing percentage of our church was getting it!

The next question measured how many people were involved in a Lifegroup. We found that 88 percent of our people attended Lifegroup two to three times a month, which meant 88 percent of our people were engaged in the main mission. Engagement in a discipleship relationship was lower, but 50 percent of the people were being discipled, and 50 percent were discipling somebody else.

Finally, we asked about sharing the gospel. We quantified it by asking, "In the last six months, have you shared the gospel in such a way that somebody could give their life to Jesus?" Amazingly, 62 percent of our people had shared the gospel in that way!

By instilling the three main values deep in our people, we saw another encouraging by-product: 75 percent of our people indicated they were tithing 10 percent of their income. What's more, 75 percent said that they were also giving above their tithe to support missionaries and other ministries around the world. Our people were living out this simple truth: where your treasure is, there your heart will be also (Matthew 6:21).

Our values were clear, and lives were being changed within our church family. We also found that God was drawing people from other places as they were watching lives being changed. One of those people was Pat Murphy.

When Pat's daughter, Brooke, showed up at Baylor, she had rejected God and the church and was living the life of a prodigal daughter. In the first semester of her freshman year, though, Brooke was miserable. She asked God to reveal Himself to her, which he did. She ultimately gave her life to Him and got involved in Antioch, where she was discipled and grew in her faith. The way Pat tells it, Brooke came home knowing God better than he and his wife, Tanya, did. "The personal, intimate relationship she had with God was something I had talked about my whole adult life but never really had," he said.

He continued, "We started looking into Antioch and heard it was a crazy church. The next time we were in Waco to see our kids, we went to visit. What we saw was not a crazy church but a whole lot of people who unashamedly loved God and had a real and dynamic relationship with God. We just fell in love with them."

God started drawing Pat and Tanya to Waco, but they weren't sure they were ready to leave behind their comfortable life. Pat had been in business for twenty-five years and was good at what he did. That success brought them a generous income and a nice life, including a vacation home and the means to travel. So when we asked him to consider coming to work for Antioch as a financial development director for a modest income, he was torn. Taking the job would mean giving up his financial independence and a comfortable retirement. Pat and Tanya had been praying, and after a night of tossing and turning, Tanya told Pat if they didn't take the position in Waco, "We are going to miss what God has for us."

So they took that step of faith, which turned out to be an important one in what God had for us as a church. Little did we know then that Pat's new role would be key in our response to an upcoming crisis halfway around the world.

> LOVING GOD, LOVING ONE ANOTHER, LOVING THE LOST.
> THESE SIMPLE VALUES LIVED OUT IN AN INTENTIONAL WAY
> BECOME THE FULL EXPRESSION OF GOD'S POWER
> AND HIS PURPOSE.

CHAPTER 14

RESTORATION VILLAGE

The Spirit of the Lord GOD is upon me,
Because the LORD has anointed me
To bring good news to the afflicted;
He has sent me to bind up the brokenhearted …
To comfort all who mourn,
To grant those who mourn in Zion,
Giving them a garland [beauty] instead of ashes,
The oil of gladness instead of mourning …
Then they will rebuild the ancient ruins,
They will raise up the former devastations;
And they will repair the ruined cities,
The desolations of many generations.

ISAIAH 61:1-4

I flipped on the news the day after Christmas in 2004 to see horrific images of destruction throughout Asia. A massive earthquake struck off the coast of Indonesia, triggering a tsunami that swept across the Indian Ocean. We would later discover that nearly 200,000 people died in one of the worst natural disasters in recorded history. The first reports seemed to indicate the extent of the damage was just a little flooding, but as the day went on we started to realize the extent of the destruction.

Laura and I began to pray that God would save peoples' lives, that the lost would be found, and that people would find immediate help. Then we began to ask, "God, what would you have us do?"

I got a phone call that afternoon from Robert Herber, our college pastor at the time. He said, "I really feel like we should go to help people affected by the tsunami. I'm ready to get a team together if you're okay with it."

Laura and I prayed about it, and I called him back to say, "Go for it. If you can get people to go, we will move heaven and earth to get them out the door with whatever is needed."

As Laura and I prayed, we sensed that we should be part of the process to get people there, but we were not supposed to go ourselves. However, as we kept praying, we both felt specifically that our daughter Abby was supposed to go. She had just turned fifteen years old and had a heart of mercy for hurting people. We sensed this was her moment. So we quickly made plans for her to go and to rally the troops around the mission that was before us.

The response from our church was amazing. There were twenty-three people who wanted to go to Sri Lanka immediately and another fifteen who signed up to go to Indonesia. Over the next month, a total of seventy-five people traveled to Sri Lanka and Indonesia. There were many more who also worked tirelessly behind the scenes to prepare, support, and send those teams.

Doctors and nurses collected box after box of medicine and medical supplies. Others provided materials and activities for children, who would be out of school and would need to gain a sense of routine and normalcy. We also began to gather food we could take in to the most devastated areas. Within two days of announcing our plans, a hundred volunteers were at our offices sorting supplies, packing boxes, and helping send people out the door.

The Man in the Maroon Shirt

On January 1, the initial team took off for Sri Lanka. When they landed, they met up with a couple of potential contacts. Their first question was crucial to setting the tone for the response: "What are your biggest needs right now?"

The local contacts pointed the team to two of the most devastated areas, one in the south and the other in the east.

The team first traveled south and began to serve a community that had not received aid. While there, they continued to receive reports of an eastern area that had minimal help. They prayed and decided to split the team in order to care for people in both places.

As they made plans to go east, it became clear that the van drivers they had hired did not want to go in. It turns out, they had a good reason. There had been a civil war going on in Sri Lanka, and a faction called the Tamil Tigers had hijacked many transports going into that area. Several van drivers turned them down before they finally found one man willing to take the trip. When asked if he would go, he replied, "Everybody has to die sometime. I'll go."

With that sense of confidence, he drove the team to a city named Kalmunai. When they arrived, they found an old hotel secure enough to hold everyone. Journalists from around the world and U.N. relief workers had already arrived, but there were no other aid groups.

Our guys slept on the floor that night and prepared to go out and help in any way they could the next day. That morning in prayer, Robert asked God for direction. He sensed God give him an image of a man in a maroon shirt. This type of experience might sound a little weird and outside our everyday experience, but when you are seeking to do the impossible, you often need a miracle to accomplish it. The team needed guidance, and they needed God to provide specific instructions on how to find it.

When they got to the coast, the team encountered total devastation. Only one building was still standing, an Assemblies of God church. As they walked toward it, a man wearing a maroon shirt walked out. With a big smile on his face, the man said, "I am so glad you're here. We have been praying for you to come. Can you help us?"

The man in the shirt introduced himself as Ravi and explained that the church was looking for a way to minister to their community. Ravi took the team to a makeshift camp where hundreds of people had gathered after the tsunami. Our team included a few EMTs who had some medical supplies with them, but the scene was overwhelming. They immediately began to clean wounds and apply first aid, but they knew it wouldn't be enough to meet the needs before them.

A man with visible injuries walked up to Robert, pleading for help. He said, "Something is wrong on the inside. I am bleeding inside. Please help me."

Robert offered the only help he could. "We don't have the supplies or ability to perform surgery, but I can pray for you in the name of Jesus," he said.

As Robert extended his hand and began to pray, his hand grew warm and the man's body began to shake. Tears began to run down the man's face, and over the next few minutes he was healed both on the inside and outside.

They were rejoicing. They were overwhelmed. Robert told the man, "God is healing your body, but He also wants to heal your heart."

"I accept!" he shouted.

"Well, wait," Robert said. "I have to tell you what you're accepting first."

As Robert unpacked the good news of Jesus, the man kept interrupting and insisting, "I accept! I accept! I accept!"

Throughout that day and evening, many people were healed through God's power, and many gave their lives to Jesus. The next day, our team went to a home where the entire family had come to faith in Jesus. It seemed appropriate to start a gathering in their home. Not only was the team loving Sri Lankans and meeting their immediate needs, but they were also connecting people together for the long haul.

Over the next week that house was filled with people, and the book of Acts came alive. Our team was able to leave the east with additions to the church, wounds healed, and the Kingdom of God moving forward.

Fighting for a Forgotten Village

Back in southern Sri Lanka, Jennifer Smyer was leading our team. When they arrived in the devastated city of Tangalle, they asked, "Are there people who are not yet being served?"

"Yes," they were told, "there are the fishermen. No one is helping them."

So the team headed to a coastal village called Moraketiya comprised of many fishermen and their families. When they found the village leader, they were shocked by what they heard. More than 800 people had been living there on the ocean's edge, and when the tsunami came, almost half of the men, women, and children were swept out to sea. In addition to physical wounds, the 450 people left behind were also grieving the loss of their children, loved ones, and entire way of life.

Our team immediately began to bandage wounds and distribute food and water. They also began to pray for them and ask Jesus to meet the needs of their hearts. The villagers were Buddhist and not open to the gospel, but they whole-heartedly received the physical help our team was able to provide.

As the days went on, Jennifer and the team came alongside the people of Moraketiya as advocates. They clearly needed homes, but they needed land first. The team went to U.N. meetings to advocate for the village to receive supplies for basic needs. They heard that the prime minister of Sri Lanka, Mahinda Rajapaksa, would be allotting land in the coming days. Jennifer and Pat Murphy, our new director of financial development, raced around to find out where the land would be. Then Jennifer, who is as bold as a lion, determined to meet the prime minister face to face and challenge him to give the village twenty-nine acres where they could rebuild.

Prime Minister Rajapaksa had come to the Tangalle area to survey the damage. After he finished speaking to representatives of various relief organizations, Jennifer immediately walked up to him.

"Mr. Prime Minister," she began, "I would like to talk with you about the people in Moraketiya."

"Oh, yes, thank you very much," he said. "You can talk to my aids."

"Actually, I would like to meet with you," she said.

He smiled and walked out, and Jennifer followed. When members of the press had gathered around him, she said again, "Mr. Prime Minister, I would like a meeting with you."

Under that kind of public pressure, he almost had to say yes. And he did. Jennifer soon met with the prime minister and his brother, who served as his senior advisor and was responsible for land distribution. They talked about the plight of the Sri Lankan people and the specific plight of poor fishing villages. The advisor said, "We will work it out for you to have this land." In that meeting he and Jennifer began to establish a working relationship that would go on for several months.

"Jennifer, what do people think of me and the prime minister?" he asked during one meeting.

"Sir," she said, "they believe you are men who understand where they come from, because you also came from a poor village."

Remembering the story of Joseph and how God put him in place for a particular hour in history, Jennifer continued, "God has placed you in this position for this time, and I encourage you to ask God to show you how to lead. It is easy to be distracted by money and power, but I encourage you to use your position for the people's good."

She told me that in that moment she could see the Spirit of God register in his eyes, with affirmation of his calling.

Twenty-Nine Acres

Jennifer and Pat set an appointment for the next week to meet with the prime minister and his brother in Colombo in order to finalize the deal for twenty-nine acres. The week before, I had received a phone call from *The New York Times*. One of their reporters had been going to camps for IDPs (internally displaced persons) in Sri Lanka. He had gone to twenty-six of them, including the one where we were working. This man didn't believe it was appropriate to mix aid work with sharing the gospel. He felt it put unnecessary pressure on people to convert in order to get the help they needed.

As he and I talked on the phone, it seemed clear that he had already made up his mind about what should and shouldn't be done. So I started asking him questions.

"Tell me about our work," I started. "Compare it to the other camps. How are our guys doing in terms of serving and meeting the needs of people?"

"It's the best work in the nation, hands down," he answered. "They're doing better work practically, meeting needs, already starting school up again, and even working through the complexities of post-traumatic stress disorder."

"Well, what's the problem?" I asked.

"The problem is you're preaching Jesus while you're doing aid work," he said.

I responded simply, "It's hypocritical not to do both because we are not two separate people. We are a people who have been loved by God, and out of that compassion we serve others. They will get aid regardless of whether they ever respond to this message of Jesus. But if we don't share Jesus, we are lacking integrity in the way we live our lives."

The reporter listened but politely disagreed. That Saturday, January 22, 2005, the front page of *The New York Times* included an article titled "Mix of Quake Aid and Preaching Stirs Concern," along with a photograph of our guys playing with the kids of Moraketiya. In the article he also quoted representatives of other Christian agencies who disagreed with sharing the gospel while providing aid.

When the article was reprinted on the front page of *The Sunday Times* in Sri Lanka the next day, it created more than a minor complication for the meeting to negotiate the land deal. Jennifer knew they would have to address this issue. The concern was that the people of Moraketiya might not receive their land because of political backlash against our group.

As she met with the prime minister's brother, Jennifer began candidly, "Obviously, you've seen the article in the paper. Do you have any questions about it? Do we need to talk about it?"

He laughed and said, "No, it sounds like that's between you and the other Christians. I'm a Buddhist. I understand. You have to live your life out of your faith. I wouldn't expect you to do anything less. I've talked to all my people. You're doing great work. Let's sign the deal. The acres are yours."

Beauty from Ashes

Those twenty-nine acres were set aside to rebuild the homes of the people of Moraketiya. They named it Restoration Village.

The mission of Restoration Village has ultimately been about the body of Christ coming together. Our whole church got behind that vision and gave themselves to it. Teachers stayed up all night writing curriculum for children who didn't have a school. Construction workers traveled back and forth, planning and building the village. Business people negotiated contracts and managed financial records. Medical personnel cared for the sick and wounded. Counselors ministered to children struggling with the incredible trauma they had experienced. More than two hundred people went out from Antioch and other churches on short-term teams. Many great men and women gave their lives generously for the people of Moraketiya.

Through the process, some incredible stories of sacrifice surfaced. One engaged couple told people they didn't want wedding gifts for themselves and instead asked guests to give to an account in order to build homes in Sri Lanka. Their sacrifice raised more than $14,000. A sixteen-year-old girl asked people to give to the Sri Lankan cause instead of buying birthday presents for her. More than $350 was received.

Antioch was not alone in the Restoration Village journey. People from all over the country, and in some cases all over the world, gave toward the project. A church in San Antonio gave $40,000. A businessman from Houston rallied support from his associates and raised over $50,000 to build the community center. A man living in Dubai, United Arab Emirates, heard about it and sent money from the other side of the world.

More than $1.3 million came in over eighteen months. We were able to completely rebuild Moraketiya debt free. There was never a time when we had to stop construction. Every time there was a need, God provided through the obedience and generosity of His people. So what did God do? A village of eighty-five homes has emerged with businesses and a developing community. God not only restored a village, He restored a people.

The most remarkable stories from the project, of course, came directly from the people of Moraketiya. In the months after the tsunami, an older fisherman shared with Jennifer, "Many people have come and gone. But your people have come and loved our children every day. They have played with our children, offered them school, and been tender with our hearts. In my culture, we hang a picture of Buddha on the wall to worship him. This makes me want to buy a picture of your God, hang him on the wall, and worship Him."

Many people came to worship Jesus as their Savior. One man shared that each night he and his wife would lay their baby down to sleep and then read the new Bible they had received by candlelight. One night, God used a dream to speak to him. He was in a deep pit surrounded by darkness and heard the voice of the Lord say, "I am the way, the truth, and the life." This man and his family are now believers who are involved in the local church that has been established there.

Long-Term Commitment

Restoration Village is a beautiful picture of true restoration—both individual spiritual restoration and physical restoration of an entire community. That kind of restoration is not the result of a quick fix or short-term solution. It takes long-term commitment to see lives healed and restored and to rebuild a village.

Our long-term team leader, Lexia, and another woman, Samantha, gave of their own finances to build a house in the village, which they moved into and served out of for the next two and a half years. Rudy, Emily, and their family also came to serve, living just outside the village. Together they served the people of Restoration Village and also reached out to the people of the larger Tangalle area. Another entire book could be written about their love and sacrifice for the people of Sri Lanka. They were not only able to leave behind a house church that has continued to grow and multiply, but there is a village and a people who have also been loved well and touched for eternity. Even today, one of our leaders from India continues to connect with and walk alongside this church in the Tangalle region.

Tragedy and disaster is a common part of living in this world. But in the midst of the pain, God has called us, the church, to be the healing and restoring grace that people so desperately need.

> THE CHURCH IS GOD'S ANSWER TO DEVASTATION IN OUR WORLD. RESTORATION HAPPENS WHEN GOD'S PEOPLE COME TOGETHER WITH THEIR UNIQUE GIFTS AND CALLINGS TO BRING BEAUTY FROM ASHES.

CHAPTER 15

THE NEXT TWENTY YEARS

Record the vision and inscribe it on tablets, that the one who reads it may run.

HABAKKUK 2:2

"Marty, grab the kids! Hurry—get everyone in the van! The mob is coming! We've got to go. Now!"

It was the summer of 2007. Our long-term team was established in Sri Lanka, and they had invited our youth group to come to do evangelistic outreaches in the area surrounding Restoration Village. This region in southern Sri Lanka contained a radical Buddhist element that was extremely resistant to seeing the church established. We were praying for a breakthrough and for our youth to have a life-changing experience, but we were not expecting a life-threatening experience!

Twenty-one youth and adult leaders traveled to a village about an hour from our hotel. Our typical outreach process was to set up in the city square, gather people, play music, perform dramas, share the gospel, and pray for people. We arrived in the village in the midst of a torrential downpour, so we gathered underneath a canopy to wait for the rain to stop. I was frustrated because we only had a small window of time, so I prayed, "God, what do I do?" It seemed to me that God clearly answered, "What do you want?"

"Well, God," I replied, "we need sunshine, and we need this rain to stop now." I prayed as I was standing out in the rain with my eyes closed. Suddenly, I felt warm sunshine on my face, and I opened my eyes to see that the rain had stopped. Within two or three minutes, the skies were clear and people started trickling back onto the streets and into the kiosks and shops. We began to gather people to hear our presentation.

After performing music and a drama, we shared the gospel. Many people raised their hands to respond to the message of Jesus. Off to the side, though, one belligerent guy was mocking our team. He had become quite a distraction. He was drunk, and he had an incapacitated hand. One of our youth tried to engage this man in conversation. As they went back and forth, the youth finally said, "Can we just pray for God to heal your hand?"

"If God can heal me, you can pray for me," came his reply. So the team prayed for the man, and as they did his immobile hand was made whole in their sight. The man began to rejoice, and it seemed as though the alcohol cleared right out of his system. It was a glorious moment as he responded fully to the gospel.

We were rejoicing in what God was doing and setting up for a new crowd that had gathered when four cars suddenly pulled up. Angry men climbed out of the vehicles with clubs in their hands. They began to grab our equipment and supplies as if they were going to take them. As I approached one of the men, the sheer intensity of his hate-filled anger stopped me in my tracks. He didn't speak English, so he turned to our translators and began threatening their lives. The angry newcomers were leaders from the Buddhist community up the road, and they seemed to be coming with a vengeance.

We immediately worked to get our team of youth into the van. It was mayhem in every direction, and I just knew that even if I survived the mob in Sri Lanka, some parent back home was surely going to kill me when news of this event got out!

We crammed everyone into one van, and as we were calling names to account for everyone, the man who had been healed walked over to confront the Buddhist leaders.

"What are you doing?" he asked. "How can you do this? These people love God. How can you do this?" And then this brand-new believer punched the Buddhist leader in the face.

Within seconds, a full-out brawl broke out, and somebody yelled, "Get the Americans!"

The mob started moving toward our van. It was absolute chaos. I screamed at one of our team leaders, "Count everybody! Make sure there are twenty-one people in the van."

Then I ran back through the streets to make sure we weren't leaving anyone behind. I was able to jump back in the van just before the mob overtook us. We drove a few miles down the road, got all the kids out, and counted heads again to make sure the whole team was there. When we got back to our hotel, the kids were going on about how cool that experience was. Of course, the leaders had a completely different perspective. We thought it had come uncomfortably close to turning into a biblical kind of martyrdom. As we gathered the youth to process the experience and look at Scripture, we realized that type of chaotic mob event happened at times when the gospel came to a city for the first time. We were stirred again by the book of Acts, realizing that the early believers experienced the same kind of encounters themselves. Of course, they had to escape by foot.

India or Home Base

For us, this trip had two purposes. We wanted our whole family to experience God moving in the nations, and we also wanted to take time to seek God about the next twenty years. Laura and I were in our mid-forties and knew we needed fresh clarity.

As we got the team on the buses headed back to the airport to fly home, our family and a few friends headed on to India to meet up with a college team in Bangalore. Laura and I were praying specifically, "Lord, are we personally called to this region of the world?" We knew that Antioch was our family and tribe for life, but we wanted to make sure we were serving from the right location.

India was in our sight for the future of our movement. Antioch had some workers in the country already, but we knew God wanted us to invest at a deeper level. More than 1.7 billion people call the Indian sub-continent home, and over a third of the unengaged, unreached people groups of the world live in this area. Laura and I have always felt called to the nations. We wanted to go, and it has been hard at times to stay behind in Waco. We needed to know: Were we supposed to put in our next twenty years in India? Were we supposed to continue from our home base in Waco?

God made His answer clear as we sought Him over the next few days: He had not called us to one specific nation or area but to *the nations*. We were to lead and look to the future from Waco. We would channel our heart for the nations by staying fully engaged in building a movement that would touch the unreached of the world.

Time to Evaluate

With this fresh direction, we gathered our leadership team back in Waco to pray about the future. We were in agreement about what we were hearing from God: *It's been twenty years since this movement started. Now I want you to pause, regroup, and look to the next twenty years.*

Over the next eighteen months, we asked for feedback from leaders outside our own movement, friends we'd known over the years, pastors, missionaries, and others who knew us. We asked for their thoughts about what they believed we should hold onto and what we should press into for the future.

We listened to our congregation. We asked ourselves hard questions. We waited on the Lord. We wanted to make sure we weren't on cruise control, simply doing the same things we had been doing. We had seen some fruit, but we knew God wanted us to experience even greater fruit in the future.

After a year and a half of evaluation, a few key pieces were clear. We were to continue to live as a people who had *a passion for Jesus and His purposes in the earth*. We were to cling to that missional, world-changing focus. We would intentionally live out simple values: love God, love others, love the lost. And we would hold onto the vision that the local church is the best mission base for reaching our city, the nation, and the world. If we would learn how do church better, then we could reproduce it at a greater rate around the world. The local church would be a mission base, much in the same way the church at Antioch was in Acts 11 and 13.

God was also speaking new things. One of the clear words that came over and over from a variety of people was the Bible story of the feeding of the five thousand. The story is a message about Jesus' heart for the masses. We were to get the message of the gospel to the masses, not just to a few.

When the disciples asked Jesus, "What are we supposed to do with these people?" His charge was, "You feed them." We could not be okay with seeing the lost around us. We, as God's co-laborers, were to be more intentional than we'd ever been before about doing whatever we could to make sure people knew Jesus.

From this feeding of the five thousand passage, we also see that one boy brought what he had. It wasn't much, but it was enough when Jesus multiplied it. God was showing us that, with Him, we had everything we needed to expand and reach more cities and nations with the message of His transforming love.

Our City

As a local church, we are called to do our part to see our city reached with the gospel and transformed with God's grace. We feel that God has promised that Waco is to be like a "city set on a hill." With renewed personal commitment and partnership with other churches, we believe we can see this promise come to pass.

In our research of the Waco area, we found there are more than 150,000 people unconnected to Jesus and His Church. That became our target. How could we do our part to see that number lowered in our city? We knew that in order to lead our movement of churches around the world, we need to be doing church better in Waco. We needed to focus on empowering every person in our church to be missional in his or her home, job, and neighborhood.

Our Nation

At the end of 2008, we had eight Antioch churches in the U.S. We were proud of the work they were doing, but through our time of seeking God we were convinced that we were called to much more.

We recommitted to plant churches in America as part of the bigger vision to reach people in the cities, our nation, and nations of the world. We wanted our churches to each become a hub of training and sending. We feel called to reach American cities, and we also feel called to mobilize them.

The Nations

Finally, we reaffirmed our commitment to the nations of the earth. What we started with are the same words we will spend our last breath on: "This gospel of the kingdom shall be preached in the whole world as a testimony to all the nations, and then the end will come" (Matthew 24:14). If there are people out there no one else will go to, our response is, "Lord, here we are, send us."

We had been fruitful, but we were longing for a greater breakthrough. Our people were sacrificing and living in some of the most difficult places on earth. They were planting churches, but they were not seeing church-planting movements.

In the summer of 2007, God connected us to Steve, a veteran International Mission Board (IMB) missionary, who was training others to catalyze rapidly reproducing movements of disciples. His stories challenged us, and his teaching from Scripture convicted us.

We came away recognizing that we had always had faith for the impossible, but we needed a process to go with it. You can have high faith and high action, but if you don't have the details, you'll never get there. You can have individual stories of transformation, but you need to attend to the details in order to build movements.

New Structures

With fresh vision we knew we needed fresh structure. Whenever you start something new, it's entrepreneurial by nature, which means allowing ministry with as much freedom as possible. We wanted to keep that same spirit but to also clarify who we are and what we do.

In response, we formalized the Antioch International Movement of Churches (AIMC) as the official network for our churches. Those who wanted to be a part of it would agree to a certain set of values, basic doctrine, and practices. It wasn't that we thought this was the only way to do things, but this network provided strength and clarity for our common goal.

A centralized structure ensures values are not compromised. A decentralized structure allows for greater innovation and leadership development. Most movements usually swing far to one side or the other. For us, we are consistently asking, "How do we keep the best of both structures?" We committed to live within that tension in order to end up with the best practices of both structures.

The X Factor

We came out of this time with lofty goals, but perhaps the biggest question was how to achieve them. We asked more than thirty of our main leaders this question: what is the one thing that, if improved, would have the greatest impact on our seeing God's promises fulfilled?

After a lengthy discussion in small groups, each came back with the same answer: *discipleship*. That would be our X factor. This was the thing that would expedite our reaching more people. If discipleship was done better, it would facilitate everything else God was laying before us.

As we were having this discussion, something dawned on me. *Oh yeah, that was Jesus' X factor, too.* I had even taught on it, but somehow I didn't recognize it until the end of our discussion. Not only was it Jesus' example, but it is also His command. He said very clearly, "Go therefore and make disciples of all the nations, baptizing them in the name of the Father and the Son and the Holy Spirit, teaching them to observe all that I commanded you; and lo, I am with you always, even to the end of the age" (Matthew 28:19-20).

If discipleship is done well, then every other area of the life of faith will fall into place. That's because discipleship teaches values. Life-on-life, intentional investment has always been the difference maker for us. It's why we've had such a large number of people involved in Kingdom work.

We knew we were to dig deep again in the area of discipleship, believing that if we would, then we would see the promises of God fulfilled in our generation—and become a legacy for multiple generations to come.

With this fresh clarity, I cast our renewed vision church-wide in January of 2009. Together, we were preparing for the next twenty years.

> GOD NEVER INTENDS FOR US TO PLATEAU PERSONALLY OR CORPORATELY. IF WE STOP AND LISTEN, WE WILL HEAR HIM CALLING US TO EVEN GREATER THINGS.

CHAPTER 16

TRUSTING GOD MORE

Not that we are adequate in ourselves to consider anything as coming from ourselves, but our adequacy is from God.

2 CORINTHIANS 3:5

What's happening? I think I'm having a heart attack!

Everything was becoming blurry, and I felt like I was going to pass out. As I pulled over to the side of the road, I cried out, "Help me, Jesus. I need You."

It was April 2009, and I was speaking at one of our churches, Waypoint Church in Omaha, Nebraska. A few months earlier in January, I had preached at Antioch about fresh vision for the next twenty years. We were in full-scale "go" mode to implement the things God had spoken, but the words I had often used with other leaders were about to come to pass in my life. *God gives the vision and then deals with the visionary.*

It had been a full and fruitful weekend in Omaha. I had finished the Sunday morning service and was getting ready for a leadership meeting when I began to have a migraine headache. I had asked to borrow a car so I could go to Wal-Mart to get some medicine. As I was driving there, my heart started racing, and I felt a pain in my chest. I thought I was having a heart attack. I pulled over to the side of the road, gasping for breath, thinking I was going to pass out. I didn't pass out, though, and I didn't have a heart attack. After a few minutes, by the grace of God, I was able to regroup and make it back to the house. I didn't want to alarm the leaders I was staying with, so I called my prayer group back in Waco and said, "Something's wrong. I don't know what's going on. Will you pray?"

My heart was racing as fast as I've ever felt it. I tried lying down to calm the racing, but it didn't stop. Still, I did another meeting that night because I'd always just pushed forward. I figured it would work itself out, but that night I couldn't sleep. The next day I flew to Knoxville, Tennessee, to be with our church leaders there and to speak at their training school for two days. When I got home, I shared with Laura and other leaders what had happened, but I was feeling a little better and felt I could keep going.

As a bit of history, I had experienced similar, milder, episodes like this since 2003. The wear and tear of life and ministry and international travel at times would cause physical stress on my body, and a mild depression would set in for a week or two at a time. Normally, after a few days off to rest, I would be able to snap out of it. But this time it wouldn't be short lived. It was a game changer.

Learning to Swim Again

On the following Sunday, I finished preaching the first of three services and felt again like I was having a heart attack. I lay down for a few minutes, got something to eat and drink, and was somehow able to finish the next two services.

The next day I had a full schedule at work. At the end of the day, I was meeting with a man on staff who happens to also be a nurse. All of a sudden I felt as if someone had turned out the lights. My body started shaking uncontrollably, and I had to lie down on the floor. I thought for sure I was having a heart attack.

With urgency in his voice, the staff member told me, "You have to go to the hospital." But I convinced him I would be fine if I could just go home and rest. By 8:00 that evening, though, I was still not fine.

I headed to the emergency room, where I stayed until 3:00 a.m. They ran every test available for a potential heart attack or stroke but didn't find anything conclusive. So they sent me home, saying, "All your vitals are fine. It must be some type of panic attack or an allergic reaction to something."

I said to myself, "Okay, whatever is going on, God has an answer. So let's seek God." Over that next week I evaluated every area of my life—physical, mental, emotional, spiritual, relational, and financial. I wanted to make sure there was no sin in my life that was causing these problems or any realignment needed on any issue. I turned over every figurative rock I could find, but my heart was still racing out of control. This led me to a series of visits to doctors, but none could identify specifically what was causing it.

I continued earnestly asking, "God, what are you doing with me?" And you know what? I didn't get an answer. What I did get, though, was the peace of God, love of God, encouragement of God, and presence of God. But I never got a word from the Lord directly related to the symptoms I was experiencing.

Our elder team has always been a place of refuge and strength for me. When I met with them, they said, "We want to give you some time off—whatever you need. We'll do whatever we need to do to allow for this." I had their full support and freedom to adjust my schedule, even taking months off if needed. The real problem, though, was that we didn't know what was going on. With kids in school and other planned activities, leaving town did not seem like an option. So I adjusted my schedule to take some time off for rest, but it's difficult to rest when your body feels out of control. That turned into many, many sleepless nights. And when sleep deprivation took place, mild depression would eventually turn into deep depression. But I was not alone.

You find at your lowest times how much people care about you. Laura, once again, became the champion of our home as she tirelessly loved the kids and me and kept us going. She listened for hours and helped me through the long nights. Without her by my side I don't know how this journey would have turned out. Even today our kids would say they felt very few effects from that time period because of Laura's strength and our close friends standing with us. The unconditional love of family and friends is how God intends for all of us to be carried in our times of need.

I also put into practice certain rhythms I had learned from helping other people with similar problems through the years. I made sure I got up at the same time every day. I spent time with Jesus declaring His goodness and memorizing Scripture. I ate three healthy meals a day and exercised daily. I made sure to stay involved with people instead of isolating myself. I did a certain amount of work every day to stay productive. Some days it seemed almost impossible to do the most basic activities, but God's grace was there to keep me going.

Late one evening after several months of little relief, I cried out desperately, "God, you have to speak to me. I can't make it. I think I'm losing my mind." As I closed my eyes and prayed, God brought an image to mind of a dark, stormy ocean. I could see myself thrashing about thinking I was going to drown. Then I suddenly realized that underneath the waves, just below my feet, was God Himself. He was telling me, "I'm not going to let you go under." The next scene flashed, and I was thrashing in the same dark ocean when the voice of the Lord said, "Stand up." When I stood up, I was in chest-high water. I could actually stand up and didn't need to thrash anymore. Then in a third scene, I was walking out of the water. Jesus was sitting on the shore. He looked at me and said, "Come sit next to Me. I want to teach you how to swim again."

As a boy I spent time swimming competitively. Swimming had been a big deal to me. God knew just the right illustration to speak to me. *I want to teach you how to swim again. Come sit by Me, and we are going to learn to do life in a different way.*

Perseverance

All of my life I had been committed wholeheartedly to whatever I was involved in. As a follower of Jesus, I became fully devoted to the Kingdom of God. I was walking with Jesus with everything I knew. I was giving everything I knew how to give. But with the increase of responsibilities and the challenges of life, I needed an increase in both the power and the sovereignty of God in my life. I needed an increased knowledge and understanding of the bigness and the breadth and the depth of God's ability—because there's only so much that I could carry on my own. Without the God factor increasing, I wasn't going to be able to lead us in this next season of our journey.

Well, the months would go on, and the challenges would remain the same. At just the right times, though, God would encourage me. Once, one of our young adults came up to me after a service and asked, "Are you okay?" I told her I'd been struggling a little, and she said, "The last three nights God has woken me up and said, 'Pray for Jimmy. Pray for Jimmy now.' So I got down on my knees, and I found myself rocking back and forth praying for you, calling out to God that He would rescue you and carry you through the night."

Tears were coming down my face. I walked away and went to my car and came undone. In the middle of the night, many times that was the exact position I had been in, kneeling on the floor by my bed rocking back and forth, saying, "God, you have to meet with me. You have to meet with me."

So many times along the way, the word of the Lord would come when I needed it. There were things I was learning, places I was going to with God that I never knew possible. But He still wasn't answering the "why" questions.

I continued to lead, although I reduced my workload significantly. I had a simple mindset: *God, I'll show up at the right place, say the right things, and do what You want me to do. I love You, I honor You, and I know You're on the other side of this. It is dark, but I know You're on the other side. So it's okay. And if I die here, I'm going to die here in faith.* I had been to doctors, and we had done what we knew to do. I didn't know what else to do but to trust Him moment by moment.

After about eighteen months of reading through the Scriptures, reading books about leaders in church history, and reading about modern-day examples of leaders who served God, I knew I was experiencing what others call "the dark night of the soul." I was encouraged that even in the darkness, God was there. I could trust God, so my goal became not to worry about what was going on in my body or heart or mind. My goal became not to worry about fears of the future or unmet expectations from the past. My goal then was simply to learn to trust Him more.

With this mindset shift, the depression slowly began to lift, but physically

I felt the same. I remember saying, "God, there is something wrong physiologically." And He spoke to me clearly: "Go talk to your doctor and ask him to pursue this deeper."

After pushing for further testing, the doctor said, "Okay, let's go with a cat scan and see if we can find something."

Within twenty-four hours of the test, I got a phone call with the instructions, "Come to my office immediately."

When I got there the doctor closed the door and said, "I'm so sorry. There was no way to have known this without that kind of testing. You were born with a unique heart defect that can definitely cause every symptom you're describing when long-term stress is added to your body."

He added, "It's been the grace of God and a miracle of God that you have made it to this point in life. Years of stress, challenge, and hard work have caused these symptoms to escalate."

While specialists were being lined up for me to consult with about my heart, I still had to get through cataract surgery, the Christmas holidays, and the kickoff of our new year. By February, I was physically crashing again. Around 11:00 p.m. one night, after Laura and the kids were in bed, I was still awake and crying out, "God, please, things have to change."

I made a phone call to my friend Ben, who was a roommate at Baylor and a pastor in Houston. He had offered to put me in touch with one of the top cardiologists in the world, the doctor who helped his dad through a heart issue. The doctor was booked six months out, but Ben said he would try to get me in. As I talked with Ben, he also asked how the stress and adrenaline issues were going. I told him they were still up and down. He asked me if I knew who the top person in the world was on that topic. I said, "Through all that I have read, Dr. Archibald Hart is the best in the world at helping people with these issues."

Ben responded, "So let's pray you get an appointment with both of these guys to get what you need."

The next morning I was sitting in Panera Bread studying for Sunday's sermon. I had a stack of books on the table, including one titled *Adrenaline and Stress* by

Dr. Hart. I got a phone call from Ben, and I stepped outside to talk with him.

"Hey, you won't believe it, but the cardiologist is willing to let you in if you can be here at 10:00 Thursday morning," he said.

I was already scheduled to be in Houston at a conference, so the timing was perfect.

When I walked back in from taking the call, a guy in the corner of the restaurant said to me, "Excuse me, but I see you're reading Archibald Hart's book. Do you know Dr. Hart?"

"No," I said.

"He was my mentor for my doctoral thesis. I'm a psychologist here in town," he said.

"Oh, what's he doing now?"

"Well, he's semi-retired, but he does meet with business leaders and pastors who have had challenges with stress and adrenaline."

"Do you think he would meet with me?" I asked. God was answering the prayer Ben and I had offered the night before.

The guy offered to email him, and within two hours, I had an appointment scheduled with Dr. Archibald Hart in Los Angeles two weeks later.

Within twelve hours God had arranged for me to meet one of the top cardiologists in the world, as well as a top expert in the field of stress and adrenaline. Both would serve to help me get back to a place of emotional and physical health.

So why did God allow me to struggle for two years? Although I may never know all the answers, two benefits from this journey are obvious. Number one, it caused me to grow deeper in my love for Jesus, and it taught me to trust Him in ways that would not have happened any other way. I hopefully now lead from a deeper place of understanding God's sovereignty and my frailty. Second, my limited ability during those years allowed many capable and strong leaders to emerge throughout our movement. Expansion of the Kingdom always rises and falls on new leaders who are equipped and released to serve larger numbers of people. I am so proud to say that our organization actually flourished and grew without me in full go mode, which is how it should be.

I used to pray before preaching, "Lord, get me out of the way so You can speak through me." Now I pray a little more softly, "Lord, change me—but please be gentle."

> IT IS THE DEALINGS OF GOD IN LEADERS' LIVES THAT ALLOW US TO KNOW JESUS MORE DEEPLY AND HELP US TO LEAD OTHERS MORE HUMBLY.

CHAPTER 17

TRANSFORMATION IN SPHERES OF SOCIETY

Therefore, we are ambassadors for Christ, as though God were making an appeal through us; we beg you on behalf of Christ, be reconciled to God.

2 CORINTHIANS 5:20

The topic was prisoner reintegration. I had been invited to a Waco city meeting to hear from Jason Ramos, a member of our congregation who was sharing his personal experience of salvation, discipleship, and restoration back into society from prison. National studies have shown that two-thirds of inmates are arrested within three years of their release, creating a major strain on society. The mayor and chief of police had called the meeting to challenge businesses, churches, and social workers to care for the thousands of convicts coming back into our city.

I was amazed as I looked around the room. Rick, a business leader and member of our church, did a presentation about his practice of employing ex-convicts. Jason, a former addict, shared his story of finding freedom in Christ and then becoming an advocate for others. Among the audience there were other members of our church, too: social workers, health care professionals, and lawyers who wanted to impact our community.

It was a wonderful picture of our heart for church members to each live out Kingdom values and look for ways to impact our city. As I sat in the meeting, it hit me afresh that our message was getting through, and we were making a tangible difference in our city.

What Is Radical Kingdom Living?

When we started the discipleship training school, we were young, passionate missionaries. We wanted to go. Anywhere. Everywhere. We fought to live a radical lifestyle and were committed to the unreached. But as our church matured, many people started to ask hard questions, such as, "What does radical Kingdom living look like if I am called to business in Texas?" or, "Is my calling as a teacher less legitimate than that of an overseas missionary?" In my heart I knew each unique vocation played a significant part in the mission of God, but I also knew we needed fresh vision to encourage and challenge our church.

The bottom line is that everyone is called to be a church planter. Through that calling, some are sent to their workplace, their neighborhood, or their classroom. Others are sent to the other side of the world. We are all called to the same thing, but the expressions of that calling are different for each of us. In fact, unless everyone does his or her part, we will not see our city transformed, nor will we see the nations reached.

Jason's Story

Jason started using drugs in middle school, which was the beginning of what turned into seventeen years of addiction. He joined a gang and dealt drugs in his teens and twenties. Eventually, he was arrested and sent to a correctional facility. In fact, it was people like Jason who caused Waco's chief of police to assert for years that it was nearly impossible to reintegrate prisoners into society.

Jason had encounters with God prior to his imprisonment, but he had never made the change those encounters demanded of him. Just prior to going back to the correctional facility for the last time, though, he fully committed himself to the Lord, knowing he had to make a change in his life. A pastor from Lubbock visited Jason in prison. He asked Jason if he knew of a church in Waco to go to once he got out. Jason remembered taking his kids trick-or-treating in 2006 and coming to a house where our children's ministry was doing music and dramas and sharing about Jesus. "Yeah," Jason said, "there is this church called Antioch that someone invited me to one time. I think I'll go there."

Shortly after he was released, Jason came to church with his son, not knowing what to expect. He felt awkward not knowing anyone, but he walked into the auditorium anyway. As he was looking for a place to sit, Amy and Jim noticed him and invited him and his son to sit with them.

Jason told the couple that he had just been released from a correctional facility and that someone had told him he should come to Antioch.

"Would you like to go to lunch with us?" Jim asked.

Amy and Jim took Jason and his son to lunch and then invited Jason to their Lifegroup. He went a few times, and then Jim and two other men in the group began discipling Jason, and they helped him find a good job.

Jason was worried about his estranged girlfriend, Monica, and their children. Now that he was following Jesus, he knew she also needed Jesus in her life. Eventually, Jason invited Monica to Lifegroup. She, too, encountered Jesus and grew in her faith through discipleship. After some time, they reunited and were married. After they got back together, Monica became pregnant with twins. Amy met regularly with Monica, gave her a baby shower, and helped the family find a rental house and move out of the projects.

Soon, Jason began reaching back into his own community, bringing other broken people to his discipleship meetings. Jim and Amy began going through the discipleship lessons with a group that met on Sunday nights in Jason and Monica's house. Jason also began working with The Feast, our Friday-night community-wide meal.

Jason began bringing people to the Lord. In fact, he was bringing whole families to the Lord and baptizing them. Over time he began small groups out of his old circle of relationships. Jason's twin brother, Jon, also came to the Lord. He got free of drugs and repeated Jason's example by going from jail to church leadership.

These two brothers had fully integrated into our church, and people started hearing their stories. The police chief became interested in Jason's story because the police department was working on an initiative to more effectively reintegrate former prisoners back into society. He asked Jason to consult with the police department as part of their efforts. He shared that because of what he saw in Jason's life, he had renewed belief that rehabilitation was possible. This is how Jason found himself sharing his testimony in front of the city government.

The mayor introduced him to the reintegration summit. It was exciting to hear Jason talk about himself as a follower of Jesus, Lifegroup leader at Antioch, husband, father, and the owner of his own landscaping business. Then he shared his entire story, from being a drug dealer and gang member to meeting God and experiencing an amazing transformation of his life through Christ. When Jason finished, the mayor returned to the podium and said, "I've never heard anything like that in my life. It's just a stunning story. Jason, if the landscaping business doesn't work out, you can just become a motivational speaker. We're all very touched by your story."

The *Waco Tribune-Herald*, our local paper, picked up on the meeting and featured Jason's testimony as the lead story later that week. His picture was front and center, and the column was filled with his story of finding Christ and being transformed through discipleship.

It struck me that our emphasis on basic values was key. If Jim and Amy had not initiated contact with Jason that first Sunday, if we didn't emphasize small groups and discipleship, if we didn't empower people in their various venues of society, Jason's story may have been entirely different.

God's Kingdom Impacts Every Sphere of Society

On the Fourth of July one year in the mid-nineties, I was in Uzbekistan with our church-planting team, and we were invited to celebrate Independence Day at the U.S. Embassy. I stepped off the dusty streets of Tashkent, went through layers of security, and suddenly found myself transported back to middle America. The smell of hot dogs wafted through the air, and country music blared through the speakers. I had stepped out of one kingdom and into another. The difference was striking.

In 2 Corinthians 5:20, God calls us ambassadors. This job title is significant, and it is given to every one of us. An ambassador is the legal representative from one kingdom to another, and the embassy is the literal soil of the home nation. If you are a believer, then you are an ambassador of heaven, regardless of your vocation. Like my experience in Uzbekistan, when people interact with you as a Christian, they experience the striking difference of stepping into the embassy of another Kingdom.

Your job might feel like a dead end, but your role as an ambassador is not. Imagine what would happen if every believer actually lived this way—if through both our words and deeds we sought to actively represent Christ to our sphere of influence. Our cities would be dramatically transformed, not by any one person but by each person doing his or her part.

Throughout history, the church has been a leader in the transformation of every area of society, from social issues such as abolishing slavery, to pioneering education for all people, to creating access to healthcare for the sick, to building godly businesses, to establishing righteous government. When the Word of God and the people of God are in sync, there is no end to seeing His Kingdom come.

At Antioch, we believe the church can change the world by changing the spheres in which we live and work. No matter where we find ourselves, God can use us to usher in His Kingdom. But it won't happen in isolation. God is going to move in every sphere of society, and He is going to do it through the church. Over the years, we have used the following diagram to capture this vision.

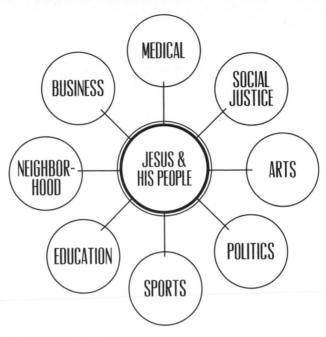

Missional Business in Waco

Business can be about more than making money—it can be about making a difference. Two of my friends bought a national mail retail franchise in order to train men and women in Kingdom business. Through the business, they train people both to work hard and to be an outlet of God's grace to the customers they serve. People who come into their stores talk about the excellent customer service and the kindness of employees. And the employees look for opportunities to pray for people and share the gospel.

In 2010, their store served people excellently and was profitable. They trained people to work hard and develop their business skills. Out of their profits they gave ten percent to missions. They also prayed for more than a thousand people, shared the gospel directly with hundreds of customers, and saw at least forty-five people make decisions for Christ. The little retail store became an embassy of the Kingdom.

It's not just business owners who are making a difference. Mark was working part time at Starbucks while in our discipleship school. He had no intention of this becoming his career, but he still felt convicted to work hard and represent Christ as an ambassador during his year there.

Mark was committed to encouraging others. He carried a positive attitude, was engaging with customers, and served his co-workers. Soon people took notice. His boss created a new position, Director of Employee Morale, and gave it to Mark. She recognized his impact and wanted to harness his influence.

Eventually, the boss told Mark that her husband could tell whether Mark had been at work that day—because he had such an impact that it affected her mood. Mark's attitude changed the atmosphere of this little Starbucks, and it changed the people around him. Not surprisingly, many of his co-workers came to Christ. They saw his work ethic, his compassion, and his life, and they wanted the same. This is the impact of an ambassador.

Missional Health Care in North Africa

The Antioch family includes many health professionals who serve our local community with compassion and excellence. It's exciting to see doctors, nurses, and physician assistants bringing help and healing to so many in our city. Not a week goes by that I don't hear of their great work. What they do in the city many times multiplies out to our work around the world. One of the ministries I get most excited about is Mental Health Grace Alliance, which was started by two church members.

A Baylor University professor named Dr. Matt Stanford is a neuroscientist whose work in the area of mental illness has been recognized nationally. His particular focus is looking at mental illness from both a clinical and biblical perspective. Joe Padilla and his wife, Jessica, served as missionaries for years through Antioch. During their years serving in Sudan, Jessica suffered with depression, which eventually led their family to return to the States for more support. Through that experience, Joe and Jessica sensed the Lord opening the door to start a nonprofit organization to serve mental health needs. They part-nered with Matt to start Mental Health Grace Alliance. Their work involves recovery support groups that integrate medical and spiritual tools for healing. They have provided hope and healing to many who had nowhere else to turn. Today, this ministry of mental health recovery and support has grown across the United States and into seven other countries, giving great relief to families in desperate need.

One of those countries is a Muslim country in North Africa. For many years, Antioch's leaders had been praying for a way to get into this formerly closed country. In 2012, this country experienced a civil war, causing the ousting of its dictatorial leader. This became our open door. We sent a team from Antioch's emergency relief arm, Acts of Mercy, to assess the needs of the people and determine how we could serve. This Acts of Mercy team found an incredible open door through the person in charge of all the medical systems in the country.

According to the medical leaders, their biggest need was for mental health, particularly tools to deal with Post Traumatic Stress Disorder (PTSD) caused by war, instability, and more than forty years of fear under a brutal dictatorship. It just so happened that Matt was an expert in the mental health field and that Joe spoke Arabic from his time in Sudan. Over the next months, those two men traveled to North Africa several times to train and set up recovery support groups for people dealing with the effects of trauma and even PTSD.

Follow-up research showed that the recovery group participants reported significantly reduced symptoms of PTSD. That, in turn, kept the door into the country open for over two years. Once again the church—Jesus' people, using their individual and combined gifts—created avenues into places that were considered closed to the gospel. Now, through Acts of Mercy, Matt has been invited to speak in many Muslim universities in that region.

When representatives from the U.S. Agency for International Development (USAID) asked which of the American NGOs was doing good work, a group of nationals named Acts of Mercy. The USAID officials asked why. "Because," they said, "many organizations talk about helping, but Acts of Mercy really does it. They've left us something substantive. They've met with us. They've trained us. And they've stayed committed."

As a result, Matt was invited to speak about our work to the United States Institute of Peace, an institution established by Congress. If Matt had not integrated his faith with his career, and had the Padillas not found God in their place of pain, we might never have been able to work with those beautiful people in North Africa.

Missional Justice

In 2011, Christine Caine, from Hillsong Church in Australia and founder of The A21 Campaign, an anti-human trafficking organization that fights slavery around the globe, came to speak at our World Mandate conference. She shared with us her heart for freeing captives, both physically and spiritually. Her message was powerful and stirred in many of our own people's hearts a desire to respond to this atrocity. We then became aware of statistics about the large number of girls being trafficked in the United States, most of them our own country's young runaways.

In response, a group of church members, under the leadership of Susan Peters, with varied skills and in different seasons of life pulled together to research and seek God's direction in ways to address the issue of human trafficking. What they found was that many young women were being trafficked right in our own backyard, through truck stops and other venues in Waco. They said, "This is not okay, not in our city. We want to be rescuers and restorers." Thus, our anti-trafficking initiative, UnBound was birthed.

There are more than twenty-seven million modern-day slaves in the world suffering under the oppression of forced labor as well as forced prostitution. This is pure evil, and it's destroying a whole generation of lives. Whenever we talk about being the church, we know we have the message that is both for the victim and the perpetrator: Jesus came to set slaves free, both inwardly and outwardly.

UnBound began to take steps by exploring various ways to abolish trafficking in our city. We started with prayer and researching what others were doing in our area. We quickly found that there was a general lack of awareness about this issue. We began compiling information on how girls were being trafficked and tricked into this industry, and we asked God to open doors to share this message. He did!

UnBound is currently collaborating with law enforcement, schools, juvenile detention centers, and businesses to train and educate on what is happening in our city. As the information is shared, especially in the schools, it is amazing to see the lights come on in teachers' eyes as they hear what potentially could be going on in their own sphere.

UnBound has also had the opportunity to be a part of a few rescues. Early on in this ministry a family contacted us to say that a young girl had been abducted and was going to be sold into Mexico. We immediately pulled together our team of lawyers, law enforcement, judges, and faithful volunteers to jump in and intervene in what was happening in this girl's life. Each person was able to do his or her part, and the girl was rescued at the last minute in a jail at the border and taken to a safe house in our state.

We are so proud of our community for coming together to fight the greatest injustice of our day. Proverbs 31:8-9 says, "Speak up for those who cannot speak for themselves, for the rights of all who are destitute. Speak up and judge fairly; defend the rights of the poor and needy" (NIV). It doesn't matter your skill set or your age— everyone is needed. I have been amazed and blown away by our team. We have had everyone from a group of carpenters and plumbers who spent more that a hundred volunteer hours to restore a safe house in our area to little kids who built lemonade stands for our "Stand for Freedom" campaign to raise money to buy the anti-trafficking curriculum we teach in schools. We have a team of lawyers giving their pro bono time helping give victims of trafficking a voice in the judicial system and college students running 5K races to raise money and bring awareness to the issue. Everyone has a place.

UnBound is now in seven states and three nations. One of our hopes and prayers is to be a part of this generation seeing slavery eradicated, and we look forward to seeing what doors God is going to open for our body as we co-labor with others. Change starts one person at a time, one church at a time.

> THE MISSION OF GOD CAN ONLY BE ACCOMPLISHED WHEN EVERY PERSON DOES HIS OR HER PART. NO ONE PERSON CAN DO IT ALL. WHEN WE ALL EMBRACE THE CALL TO LIVE AS AN AMBASSADOR OF CHRIST, THERE IS NO LIMIT TO WHAT THE CHURCH CAN DO.

CHAPTER 18

CALLED TO OUR NATION

But you will receive power when the Holy Spirit has come upon you;
and you shall be My witnesses both in Jerusalem, and in all Judea and Samaria,
and even to the remotest part of the earth.

ACTS 1:8

Boston, Massachusetts, is not the same as Waco, Texas. Our first church plant in the United States found that out the hard way. We had always taught that if you can learn to do church here in Waco, then you can do it anywhere. Yet while the basics of the Kingdom do work anywhere, it's not always easy to reach a completely different culture.

We had been sending teams to the nations for five years when Sean Richmond, our youth pastor, challenged us that we were also called to our own nation. As we prayed together, we realized that in the same way God had called us to the remotest parts of the earth, He had also called us to the United States. God was leading us to be a part of seeing the age-old foundations restored in our nation so that a new generation would come to know Jesus and to be trained and equipped to change the world.

So Sean and his wife, Laura, packed up and moved to Boston in January 1998. The rest of the team joined them in September to start our first U.S. church plant. We thought it would be easy because it was in the United States, but it took a while for a bunch of Texans to understand Boston culture and how to effectively reach people from the East Coast. Eventually, though, they began leading people to Christ and teaching them the basic values of the Kingdom. Together, they formed a new church called Community of Faith Christian Fellowship, which carried the values of loving God, loving others, and loving the lost.

They have now planted two other churches in different areas of the city, as well as planting Antioch Community Church in Tempe, Arizona. From Boston, they have sent long-term missionaries to work in seven different countries. Their example has encouraged our faith that other cities in our nation can also become a base of planting churches and training and sending people to the nations.

Why the U.S.?

Initially I wrestled with the idea of planting churches in the States. On the one hand, I knew from Acts 1:8 that the church is called to reach the whole world. On the other hand, I had a hard time justifying sending laborers to American cities already filled with hundreds of churches while Muslim, Hindu, and Buddhist areas of the world were lacking even one Christian missionary to serve millions of people. Yet we sensed God's leadership to send laborers to the U.S., and we came to understand that we needed to take ownership of our nation, too.

Each new church would become a base to train and send more laborers into the harvest field—their own city, our nation, and the nations of the world. By 2007, we had started seven churches, and a few of those were planting other churches. By the end of 2013, we had quadrupled the number of our church plants in the States. With our training and development processes in place, we have great expectations to see many more planted in the near future. Now, thousands are gathering in Antioch churches across our nation in addition to the original church in Waco. As we look to the future, Antioch churches in our nation, will be collectively responsible for sending out far more missionaries to the unreached than we ever could have from just one church in Waco, Texas.

All People's Story

This is Robert Herber's story of God's call on him and his wife, Stefanie, to church planting in the United States. It's just one example of our many great men and women who have been called to do the same.

I was leading the college ministry at Antioch Waco when Jimmy asked me to pray about committing to help develop the U.S. church-planting side of the Antioch movement for the next ten years. One day, I was on my knees, asking God if this was what He had for me for the next decade. God clearly affirmed my call to church planting. But his next words surprised me: in San Diego, California. Honestly, I didn't even know where San Diego was in California. I actually got off my knees and walked over to a globe in the room. When I saw it was a port city that bordered Mexico, I got excited because my heart was always to plant churches in ethnically diverse cities.

After praying with the elders of Antioch, they agreed we had a true call to pioneer a church in San Diego. As I began to pray about what this church would be like, God clearly gave me a name for it: All Peoples Church. By God's grace we would plant a multi-ethnic church in the heart of one of America's most diverse cities. Revelation 7:9 was the biblical basis for the church's name: "After these things I looked, and behold, a great multitude which no one could count, from every nation and all tribes and peoples and tongues, standing before the throne and before the Lamb, clothed in white robes, and palm branches were in their hands"— but God showed us that our theme verse would be Luke 4:18-19: "The Spirit of the Lord is upon Me, because He anointed Me to preach the gospel to the poor. He has sent Me to proclaim release to the captives, and recovery of sight to the blind, to set free those who are oppressed, to proclaim the favorable year of the Lord." In this verse, Jesus defines His ministry as one to the poor, the captives, the blind, and the oppressed. To the least of these, He would bring His good news.

We might have had a clear calling and a clarion mission state-

ment, but that didn't mean our journey would be easy. No matter how hard we tried, Stefanie and I could not secure housing for our family. This was particularly challenging because we sold a beautiful home in Waco and had given almost all of the money toward ministry to the poor. On the day of our departure, all we could say to the guys in the moving truck was to drive to San Diego and await our instructions.

My family landed in a hotel in a shady part of town. Our first night in the city, I was broken. We had no home and no connections. That night, I stood looking out the window at strip joints and bars and then at my wife and young children, who had been pulled away from their full life in Texas. I felt like a fool. As I voiced my complaint to God, I sensed this response: I have brought you here to be a part of a great revival here in this city. Oh, how I needed to hear those words that night.

Soon, a large house opened up less than a block from the campus of San Diego State University (SDSU)—in the middle of a cluster of wild party houses. The day we pulled up with our moving truck, a girl approached me to ask why I would move my little family into this environment. I found out later she thought I was an undercover cop coming in to bust up all the drug activity happening in the school's party scene. Within the first two months of our time in the neighborhood, cops busted a drug ring of seventy-five students who had been smuggling drugs from Mexico. Just minutes from our house, a student was also murdered. When I told this girl that I had come to start a church that was about relationship with Jesus, she said she was blown away. She told me she was not a God follower, but she had been wondering what God was like and if He wanted a relationship with her. Within a month, she had accepted Christ as Lord and Savior.

This young woman was an athlete at SDSU, which would open a huge door for us. She and her three roommates lived in a popular party house where other athletes liked to hang out. One of the girls *was dating the captain of the football team, and another was dating the most popular baseball player. Soon God was working miracles. As the girls observed our lives and came into our home, one by one they would comment on how different we were. Each of them came to Christ. Next, I began to disciple the baseball player. This opened the door to share with other baseball players, and several came to Christ. Soon I was asked to lead devotions for the Aztec baseball team.*

Eventually, the fourth roommate came to Christ.

One day as I walked across campus, the football captain, Russell, stopped me. I thought he might be coming to beat me up because I was ruining the party house as one by one the girls living there were coming to Christ. But instead, Russell asked if he and Alli, his girlfriend, could come over to talk with Stefanie and me. When we sat down together, they said they wanted what we had in our lives, and right there Alli accepted Jesus, and Russell rededicated his life to God. I had been praying for them for four months.

Within the next month, one of the school's craziest party houses became the meeting place of one of our first Lifegroups. Russell ended his football season by standing up and preaching to his whole team about how God had changed his life and how they could know Jesus personally.

Soon these athletes were going with us to the inner city to share the gospel. These guys were great at building relationships with the skaters, gang members, prostitutes, and homeless. Quickly my house was packed out with about fifty young adults of different ethnicities and economic levels, mostly from non-believing backgrounds. By God's grace, within the first eight months, more than a hundred people came to faith in Christ.

Now, almost six years later, we are a church of about a thousand people meeting house to house and on Sunday mornings in our city. We are an ethnically diverse church, with more than twenty nations represented. Our services are translated from English into both Span-

ish and Swahili, and we have begun to send out missionaries to Thailand, Brazil, and Dubai, with workers preparing to go to India, Japan, and Peru.

It Can Happen Anywhere

Many would say Boston and San Diego are two of the most secular and unchurched cities in America, yet we have seen a reproducing church planted in each of them. We now have Antioch churches coast to coast.

We believe it is the hour for a new move of God in our nation. God is moving through all kinds of churches across our country. He is renewing the existing churches and stirring many new movements of church planters. We at Antioch want to join alongside and believe for hundreds of churches to be planted in cities across our nation.

Our nation was started by a group of people who believed that God and the Bible are the centerpiece not only for building our personal lives and families, but also for building a nation. Throughout American history, the renewal of the church and the planting of churches have directly correlated to the flourishing of healthy families, businesses, governments, and other institutions of society. Even today as you drive across America, in the center of each city, you will find churches. In 1 Timothy 3:15, the Bible calls the church the "pillar and support of the truth." When the church is being the church, America has hope; when the church wanes from being the centerpiece of society, we see decay in every area of life. May these be great days of seeing the church come alive in America to see renewal in our own country and to once again become the greatest missionary sending nation of all time.

EVERY GENERATION NEEDS A NEW GENERATION OF CHURCH PLANTING. WE NOT ONLY NEED RENEWAL IN OUR EXISTING CHURCHES, BUT WE ALSO NEED NEW CHURCHES TO EMERGE THAT WILL SAVE THE LOST, EQUIP THE BELIEVER, AND EMPOWER THE CHURCH ONCE AGAIN IN ITS MISSION.

CHAPTER 19

REACHING A NATION IN SHOCK

The LORD will guide you always;
he will satisfy your needs in a sun-scorched land
and will strengthen your frame.
You will be like a well-watered garden,
like a spring whose waters never fail.
Your people will rebuild the ancient ruins
and will raise up the age-old foundations;
you will be called Repairer of Broken Walls,
Restorer of Streets with Dwellings.

ISAIAH 58:11-12 (NIV)

On January 12, 2010, a devastating 7.0-magnitude earthquake shook the nation of Haiti to its core. As we began to see images on television of the mass devastation, we knew we had to respond. We already had trained volunteers for disasters like this, and we were ready to go. Kevin Johnson, our international director, pulled together a team of doctors, nurses, counselors, and support personnel. They flew out the morning of January 17, landed in the Dominican Republic, and drove to the border to cross into Haiti.

At the border they met absolute devastation, and our doctors immediately kicked into gear. People were being carried to an outpost there, and within minutes of arriving, our doctors were doing surgeries and even amputations right there in MASH-type hospital units. The next morning, they headed to Port-au-Prince, where the greatest destruction had taken place. We had a contact at a Christian school that was facilitating small organizations that were willing to come. Through coordination meetings each morning, they would identify places in need of medical care. The team would then rent vehicles and drive out to these areas, where they would create makeshift triage tents using tarps and PVC pipes. Our guys were working day and night, mending wounds and saving lives.

Heartache in Haiti

Immediately after our team left, Laura and I realized that in order to be advocates for the work, we needed to be a part of it as well. We decided to meet up with the team in Port-au-Prince. After making a couple of phone calls, Laura and I were scheduled to meet a group at 3:00 a.m. at Fort Worth's Alliance Airport. The airplane we would be flying on had been leased by Ross Perot. His son-in-law, who is a surgeon, had outfitted this airplane with pallets of medical and aid supplies. We got the last two seats on the plane, traveling with doctors and nurses from around the country who were compassionately responding to this disaster.

When we landed in Port-au-Prince, we spent a few hours unloading these pallets by hand. When they understood the work we were doing, they gave us $200,000 worth of medicine and supplies our guys needed to continue their work. As Laura and I drove through the streets, we were moved to tears seeing people living on the median in the middle of the street, under tarps and cardboard boxes. We could see X's spray painted on houses where people had died. Everywhere we went, we saw devastation.

It was midday when we arrived at Quisqueya Christian School, and our team was out in the city at work. That evening, as our teams got back, they recounted the events of the day: the burn victim they life-flighted with a Navy helicopter, the child who would have died without medications, the number of sutures they did, and the trauma counseling they were able to provide. I was in awe at the incredible work our team was doing. As we started to piece it together, we realized we were a part of something much bigger than just relief work. We were a part of God's heart to reach out to a nation in pain.

At the school we were based out of, many relief groups from around the U.S. slept in school rooms and in tents on the grounds. It was incredible to see the sacrifice of so many there to serve people they had never met. Each evening, we would sit in coordination meetings, and the teams would identify places in the city where no food, water, or medical attention had arrived. The leaders would assign teams to different areas based on their skills, abilities, and willingness. We had an incredible team of doctors, nurses, and assistants who were willing to go anywhere and do anything.

The next morning Laura and I loaded up with our team. We drove over an hour to an area of town that looked like it had been bombed. Our team of fifteen took our supplies and personnel and set up a makeshift medical unit in the middle of a demolished neighborhood. The people came in droves, desperate for help. The line of people waiting for care was more than two hundred deep. While the medical team saw patients, Laura and I and others did triage, ran a makeshift pharmacy, and followed up with prayer and counseling after they were treated. After a couple of hours, I realized the line was still very long, and the people were weary and in need of encouragement. I decided to go out and preach the gospel to the line of people, to tell them about the love of God and pray for them. Maybe God would do a miraculous healing even as they were waiting for the medical attention. As we shared the gospel, many people responded with tears of pain as well as a desire for Jesus. Others were touched by the power of God with healing and restoring of their bodies.

As I walked back to the tent after sharing the gospel, one of our doctors said, "Man, it blesses me so much to hear you preach the gospel." I was overtaken with emotion as I looked at this doctor who had worked tirelessly for three days straight, sacrificing so that people could be healed and restored. Tears welled up in my eyes as I said, "I love watching you *do* the gospel."

You see, when Jesus talks in Acts 1:8 about being a witness, that word *witness* has two meanings. One is the message we speak, and the other is the life we live. Everything about the Kingdom of God is both a declaration and a lifestyle.

That evening after the debriefing, Kevin and I prayed together, "God, what are you saying for this nation?" We both had such a deep sense that this nation needed people to be committed to it. Haiti had been a devastated place before the earthquake, and now its pain was even greater. We felt Antioch was to commit to five years: first to immediate relief and then to reconstruction and development for the future.

Rebuilding

And so began our journey.

For the next eleven weeks, we sent thirteen consecutive teams to offer medical care and relief to communities devastated by the earthquake in Port-au-Prince, Petit-Goâve, and Leogane. The impact of the earthquake was almost unquantifiable. Everywhere we looked there was concrete rubble lasting for miles, broken up by seas of tarps and tents where people had begun to relocate. It was obvious that this would be a long road to recovery. As our assessment team was on the ground in March, God orchestrated a few significant connections with different individuals, which ultimately led to a meeting with the mayor of Leogane. The mayor led our team to a small community called Lafferronay, which had yet to receive any significant support. At that point, more than a hundred families were living in tarps and tents in a field that was normally used for playing soccer and drying laundry. We knew that our greatest ability to help as a church was to do as we had done in Sri Lanka: take a small community, love it thoroughly, and love it well. Hopefully it would be an example to other communities and organizations of what God could do.

The obvious initial need was shelter, so we committed to support the construction of new homes for families who needed to resettle back into their neighborhood. From the beginning, our commitment was for members of this community to be at the forefront, not the background, of the restoration effort. We worked closely with local leaders and hired a construction crew of twenty-five masons and carpenters from Lafferronay instead of bringing in teams to do the work for them.

Every family who received a home also played an integral role in the process by clearing land, bringing water, and painting their home. Over the next year, the community became partners rather than recipients. When they asked what we would do for them, we responded by asking them how *they* wanted to serve their community. Not only did we see one hundred and nine homes built through Acts of Mercy, but we also partnered with another agency called World Renew to see sixty-five more homes go up as a result of assessments we had conducted in the community.

Before we had access to rubble removal machines, the community leaders formed a community work day. Together, we pulled rubble from destroyed houses and pounded it into holes in the road that the earthquake caused, making it difficult for children to walk to school. Later, we partnered with other organizations for rubble removal, latrines for every home, water wells, and better irrigation canals.

One of the most effective short-term programs we hosted was a trauma care group for the community. Over four months, people had a safe place to voice their grief and their fears, learn practical ways to deal with PTSD, and come together as a support for one another.

Volunteer relief coordinators from our church left their jobs from six weeks to four months to walk with this community and host short-term teams. In the meantime, people in the U.S. were signing up to join our long-term team and starting to raise financial support for their time in Haiti.

One of the most beautiful parts of this process was seeing the incredible collaboration that took place. Churches all across the Antioch movement sent teams and volunteers; other organizations filled in the gaps by clearing rubble, drilling wells, and providing trauma counselors; and, most importantly, the community of Lafferronay gave their time and skills even as they healed.

In February 2011, our long-term team began to arrive in Leogane. As the initial relief activities were winding down, we started looking toward longer-term development activities and identified churches to partner with.

Our commitment from the beginning was to strengthen local leadership and mobilize the local church to affect every sphere of society and ultimately to see their region transformed spiritually, physically, and socially. We began investing in several churches that were strong in evangelism and corporate prayer but needed help in discipling its congregation in a life-on-life way. We also started initiatives that invested in leaders who were impacting different sectors, such as health and education, as well as community leaders who could initiate community development changes.

Erika's Story

Kate, a physician assistant from Texas, began working in a local clinic serving four schools and several communities alongside two Haitian nurses, Marise and Berline. Kate met with them to teach lessons on basic healthcare principles and techniques, as well as to study the Bible and learn to make disciples. Erika Kraus, our director for Haiti Transformed, shares the following story:

> Not only were the nurses ecstatic to gain practical skills, but they were also so blessed to receive spiritual encouragement. When an eight-year-old girl from one of the schools was involved in a tragic car accident that left her in a coma and with broken legs, Nurse Marise and Kate would visit the hospital every day to pray with her family. At that time the girl's family was primarily practicing voodoo and was not open to the gospel, but they were hurting and in need of encouragement. Miraculously the girl came out of her coma, and Nurse Marise called her family daily. One day she

led the mom to the Lord over the phone. Since then, the girl has fully recovered, and her other family members have given their lives to Jesus as well.

Marise not only invests in the lives of students and families, but God has also increased her boldness to minister to her own neighbors and family members. This investment in two women has grown into a larger group of nurses throughout all of Leogane who completed our clinical mentorship course and are now meeting monthly to pray for and encourage one another, as well as to grow in their clinical skills.

As we continued to learn how to bridge evangelism, discipleship, and community development, we launched a program called the Integrated Community Health Initiative (ICHI). This equips local community development trainers to empower churches and committees to rally community members around sustainable development. The current leader of this initiative is Amos, a Haitian who was pulled out of the rubble barely alive after the earthquake. He, along with many others, was completely devastated by the destruction of their village, even to the point of despair and clueless about how to move forward. Amos joined our team in 2011 as one of twenty-six volunteers to work on rebuilding the area. He has had a heart change from being one who depends on free aid-based structures to help people stay alive, to believing that people can partner with God to find solutions to make change.

The village of Lafferronay has experienced the gospel both in word and deed. The school is up and running, they have access to the medical care they need, and they have learned to work hard in being a part of the process of the practical reconstruction of their village. But most of all, they have not only heard the message of Jesus, but many have also embraced it as the centerpiece of their lives.

In the early days, one of the leaders of Lafferronay pulled me *aside and said, "We have heard about Jesus all our lives, but nobody has taught us how to walk with Jesus. The Acts of Mercy team is not just teaching us how to pray but how to live."*

Today, our long-term team, made up of families and single women from our churches, continues to live out the gospel among the people of Lafferronay and the surrounding communities. Haiti Transformed was birthed from the church simply being the church. When a healthy church takes responsibility for world evangelization, we can't help but use every gift possible to see hurting lives restored.

WE ARE NOT JUST CALLED TO TELL PEOPLE ABOUT JESUS; WE ARE CALLED TO WALK WITH THEM IN EVERY AREA OF THEIR LIVES. THE GOSPEL IS NOT JUST WORDS BUT ALSO ACTIONS.

CHAPTER 20

BREAKTHROUGH IN THE MUSLIM WORLD

Other seeds fell into the good soil, and as they grew up and increased,
they yielded a crop and produced thirty, sixty, and a hundredfold.

MARK 4:8

Tears were streaming down my face as I shared with Nadia* the love of Jesus and how much He cared for her. The tangible presence of God was in the room. She also began to cry as we talked about His sacrifice and forgiveness for us all. As I finished sharing, I asked if she was ready to give her life to Jesus.

"No," she said matter of factly, "I'm a Muslim."

I was shocked. Never before had I sensed God's presence so strongly and shared Jesus so deeply without a response. This was different.

It was the late 1990s, and I was visiting our team in the middle of a war-torn country in the Middle East. There, they had befriended Nadia and her husband, who were both influencers in their community. The team had loved them, shared the gospel with them, and lived out the gospel among them. This woman was warm and kind, but she had not yet crossed the line to faith in Christ. She understood who Jesus was and even believed His story, but she was not ready to give Him her life. The team had asked me to meet with her and to talk in depth about her faith.

After she left that evening, I talked to the team about my experience. With broken hearts they told me there was a blindness, a barrier, something strong that was blocking her from responding to this message. Something that was warring for her soul.

Our teams working among Muslims over the past twenty years have given their lives for the people they love. They have shared the gospel countless times. They have lived the gospel in practical ways, and they have cared for the poor and the sick. They have been friends and neighbors. Our teams working with Muslims have been some of our best missionaries. But they have seen the fewest number of disciples.

I realized this was not just our problem. Across the Muslim world, missionaries for years had experienced this same reality. We needed a breakthrough.

Noah's Story

The first Antioch team to move to the Middle East involves a story of perseverance. They lived through a war, one couple lost a child to SIDS, their families' lives were often in danger because of violence, and eventually the whole team was kicked out of their country. In addition to the suffering, they did not see even one person become a true disciple of Jesus during their first seven years. Most would have quit, but they stood on the promise of God and continued to fast and pray for breakthrough. As they moved to a neighboring country, they began to see a few people come to faith and begin to follow Jesus.

One outreach strategy was to participate in media follow up. For example, a Christian radio program airing in the Middle East received many responses from people who say they want to follow Jesus. They would give us some of those names to follow up with. This work was not without risk both for the locals calling in and for our team making the follow-up calls. But our team was willing to take the risk as they yearned to find people hungry for Jesus.

One day in November 2010, we were told that there were two contacts who needed follow up, and we could choose which one we wanted. One contact was a nice sounding older man, and the other was a fiery, passionate younger guy. Given the personalities involved, it would have been normal to choose the young guy. However, while praying, the Lord specifically spoke to our coordinator to follow up with the older man.

This sixty-four-year-old man, Noah* was from a Druze background and had become a believer by watching Christian broadcasting channels. He had been studying the Bible for about four years, despite the fact that he had strong Islamic training and had memorized the Qur'an, the Muslim holy book. He had been a political and government leader in the past. Christian television evangelists had convinced him of the truth of Christ, and through revelations of truth from the Holy Spirit, he responded and had gathered twenty-one others around him who believed like he did.

He eventually called the radio station for help after visiting eleven local churches to ask for help growing in his faith. Others were reluctant to offer Noah help because they knew his background and feared persecution. Upon talking with our team, Noah said, "For two months I've been trying to find Christians to help me. They're scared of me because I'm a Muslim Arab and a political leader, and they won't help me. So are you going to help me or do I need to find someone else?"

Tim, one of our team members, responded quickly, saying, "Of course I'll meet with you."

Tim and our team leader, Paul, began to meet consistently with Noah. They were ecstatic to find someone who was serious about wanting to follow Jesus with his whole life. In their first meeting they told Noah they would never teach him anything that was not directly from the Bible. They agreed that whenever they had questions, they would all go to the Bible and not just spout opinions. They covenanted that the Holy Spirit and the Scriptures would be the centerpiece of their journey. In the first month, Tim and Paul had the privilege of baptizing Noah and his eldest son. Tim's wife also baptized one of the female leaders. They in turn went out and began to baptize the new believers.

Paul, Tim, and our team had spent years refining evangelism tools and foundational teachings to help Muslims come to Jesus and be discipled. They told Noah they would teach him one Bible lesson at a time, but then he would need to go and teach others. Not only was he motivated, but he actually would end up being more zealous than they ever could have imagined.

Over a month, those original twenty-one disciples would multiply to forty, and the movement continued to multiply month after month from there. Eight months later, there were 1,200 baptized followers of Jesus. As in all movements of God, both historical and biblical, Tim, Paul, and their team, would work through the normal challenges of leadership, purity, and biblical clarity with Noah and the early leaders. Problems often paralyzed growth, but every time they would work through a situation, the movement would then begin to grow again exponentially. Powerful Acts-like stories began to emerge, including people having dreams and visions of Jesus and miraculous healings taking place. With the miracles and growth came persecution, first in small ways and eventually escalating to the point that our people's very lives were in danger.

Since that initial meeting with Noah in 2010, the movement continues to grow. Noah and some of the original leaders have dealt with much persecution and have had to flee the country. They have handed the work over to multiple leaders who continue to reach out, disciple, and baptize men and women who are seeking freedom and truth.

Paul, his wife, Ruth, and our original team went to the Middle East in 1999 with the promise of God from 1 Peter 2:9-10. After fifteen years of labor, love, and sacrifice, they were seeing the incredible move of God they had prayed for: "But you are a chosen race, a royal priesthood, a holy nation, a people for God's own possession, so that you may proclaim the excellencies of Him who has called you out of darkness into His marvelous light; for you once were not a people, but now you are the people of God; you had not received mercy, but now you have received mercy."

Mark's Story

Meanwhile, in the northern part of that country, a college student from Texas came to spend the summer with our team. One day as she was mistakenly walking through a dangerous neighborhood, a taxi driver who had recently been in America decided he should help get her out of the area.

While in the taxi, she saw an opportunity and shared the good news with the driver, whose name was Mark*. She asked if he was a Muslim. He replied, "In my heart no, I am not. I want to follow Jesus truly in my heart."

A team member followed up with Mark a few days later and discovered that he was truly hungry for God. While they were meeting to share Jesus with Mark, he would leave to perform the salat, the Muslim ritual prayer, and then return to learn more about Christ. For months it seemed that no one else from Mark's family was interested in Jesus. Frustrated, our team asked Mark if he had any friends who might be interested in the gospel. He responded by saying, "Of course. Several of them have already accepted Christ, and I am teaching them the same things you have taught me."

They started teaching Mark about baptism, encouraging him to be baptized in the presence of some of his friends. Finally, Mark and two of his friends were baptized in a public pool at a popular tourist site for locals. After the baptism, the power of the Holy Spirit became very real to them and ignited their faith. They began to speak with a new boldness about Jesus. The movement began to multiply rapidly from a few to hundreds and into the thousands. The team taught the same things to Mark and the other leaders that they had taught Noah—and the movement continued to grow.

Because of the war in Syria, many Syrian refugees had fled to this country to find refuge until things settled down. Mark met a refugee while shopping and shared Jesus. This Syrian man accepted Christ and soon began to share and teach others himself. Quickly, there was a group of a hundred believers. When these new believers recognized the implications of the gospel, they were determined to take the good news back into the war zone they had just escaped. The fledgling church took up an offering and was able to buy bus tickets to send these new believers home. We have since heard reports of hundreds in Syria coming to faith, alongside reports of severe persecution.

One day Mark and a few friends approached our team and asked them to name the most difficult Muslim nation to reach. Within days, these three young men were on the road headed to that Middle Eastern country. There, three men came to Christ and were baptized. Once they had been baptized, taught, and trained, they also began sharing the gospel. The movement in that country is about three hundred strong and is growing rapidly.

Already this movement of Arab Muslims coming to faith is a part of a movement of God across the Arab world. Persecution is beginning to rise up against them, but the people of God are standing in the face of it. When we experience New Testament power, we will also see New Testament persecution. Our prayer is for all believers who are suffering for their faith to trust that God will meet them in their situation with His presence and peace. We are asking God that the result of their plight would be the spread of the gospel. We know from history that God will work all suffering together for good. Persecution, when rightly responded to, will take the movement in the Middle East to a whole new level, just as it did with Christianity in the first century.

Muslims for the Master in Lebanon

Our people who work in the Muslim world are doing it in a holistic way. They are winning Muslims' hearts by caring for their lives. When your gospel message is not just words but actions, lives are changed.

Sam and Julie went to Lebanon in January 2004 with a team of nine. They were ministering in a large city among Shiite Muslims. They were able to see a house church started and many people give their lives to Jesus. In 2006, there was a short war between Israel and Hezbollah, which caused people to flee for refuge to different parts of the country. At that time there were 700,000 Shiite Muslims living in the southern part of the country whose villages and lives had been turned upside down. Because of the great need, Sam and Julie and other team members started to spend two to three days a week in the south hosting medical clinics, providing food and clothing, and caring for the shell-shocked and mourning villagers. They were welcomed with open arms by families who were very grateful for the help.

During the next months they would not only fall in love with these people, but they would also move their family to the southern area of Lebanon. They chose a small, struggling village as their base of ministry. They only had electricity two to six hours a day, but they made it their home because they knew this was where they were needed.

During their time there they would establish a medical clinic, a school for children, and a job-training program for the poorest of the poor in southern Lebanon. Loving their neighbors, they began to gain favor—people were coming to Jesus and house churches were beginning to emerge. As was the case in other countries, finding the kind of man or woman of peace we find in Luke 10:5-9 would be the key to the gospel spreading.

One of them, a man called Karem*, would become a marvelous friend and partner in spreading the gospel. After coming to Jesus, Karem had led many of his family members and friends to faith. Sam continued to invest in Karem, and they became partners in sharing the gospel with others. Karem's job would take him traveling around the southern part of the country. Sam would often ride with him on the pothole-riddled roads and would pick up locals who needed rides along the road. They talked to them about Jesus and gave them Bibles and copies of *The Jesus Film*.

One day they picked up a man named Mohammad*. Sam ended up praying for him in the car, and Mohammad told him, "I feel peaceful and happy. What is that?"

Sam told Mohammad, "That is the Holy Spirit touching your heart because He loves you and wants you to know that Jesus isn't just a prophet or the head of some religion. What we have been telling you about Him is true."

Mohammad responded with, "Inshallah," which means "God willing." Sam responded, "No, really, it is true. Jesus is the Messiah, and God really loves you!"

Three weeks later, Sam took Abdullah, another young believer he had discipled, with him to visit Mohammad at his mechanic shop. Mohammad had a broken shoulder from a few weeks earlier and had recently torn the tendons in both arms from falling into the mechanic pit. When Sam and his friend arrived, they shared stories about Jesus from the Bible and then asked Mohammad if they could pray for him. After they had prayed in Arabic for about a minute, they asked Mohammad if he felt better. He sat motionless, smiling for a moment and then said, "I feel happy and peaceful but I still feel pain." They asked him if they could pray for him again. After about thirty seconds more of praying, Mohammad jumped up and shouted, "What did you do, what did you do?"

His smile reached from ear to ear as he started to move and twist his arms. "Alhamdulillah!" he yelled. "Thanks be to God! I am healed! Jesus has healed me!" He picked up a car door and repeatedly lifted it above his head, shouting with joy.

Mohammad erupted, "Jesus, I believe! You are the Lord and Messiah. You are real, and I want you in my life. I give you my life."

He had tears in his eyes and a smile on his face, as did Abdullah and Sam. He then began shouting and pointing out to the street, "I love Jesus! I want to follow Him. I have to tell everyone about Him. I have to tell my family. I have to tell my brother! I have to tell my whole village—everyone!"

Over the coming days, Mohammad's story of healing by Jesus spread to people throughout the surrounding Hezbollah villages, including the doctor who confirmed the healing the next day. Although great persecution followed with his own family and friends, Mohammad stayed faithful to His Lord and continued meeting in his house with anyone who would come. Stories like this continue throughout Lebanon as God is at work through dreams, visions, healings, and courageous men like Mohammad and Karem.

The Maga People of Indonesia

Not only is God moving in the Middle East, but He is moving among Muslims around the world. In Indonesia, western missionaries have been sharing the gospel with the Maga*, for the past three hundred years. The Maga are a people group of eight million Muslims who have been aggressively resistant to the gospel. Our people and many others had been praying for this group for years, and they were about to see real fruit.

Two of our team members went out on a Thursday afternoon to share the gospel among the group of unreached Muslims who were trash collectors by trade. Two men responded to the gospel, and our team gave them Bibles. A few days later, one of our team members went back to follow up and baptize these new believers. One of the men, Ahmed*, had a dramatic deliverance from years of witchcraft after being baptized. The change in his life was so powerful that he began to share the gospel boldly even in the face of persecution from his own village.

After we he had not seen Ahmed for a few days, our team member who was discipling him became concerned. Anxiety melted when Ahmed eventually showed up and said he had met a family from the Maga people. He had shared Jesus clearly and boldly, and the whole family gave their lives to Jesus. Their conversion brought on serious persecution, so they fled to one of the other Indonesian islands.

Ahmed visited and discipled this family. This led to twelve more Maga families coming to the Lord on their new island home. Shortly after this, these new believers were taken down to a river to be baptized. The river water flowed under a thick forest of trees covering the river. Many friends of these families came to watch the watery event. As they all stood in witness, out of nowhere blew a strong wind through the area, moving the trees. Those watching came under awe and conviction from God, which resulted in nine more families coming to the Lord and being baptized. With this outbreak of new life came another wave of persecution. Seven of those families' homes were burned to the ground by angry Muslim mobs, and again this new group of believers fled to another island.

Like Peter, these Jesus followers were fishermen by trade. When they arrived on the new island, the people told them the fishing had been meager, and there was not enough for all of them to fish there. The faith-filled believers prayed as they worked and would come in with their nets overflowing with fish. Word spread, and more than five hundred people eventually gave their lives to Jesus and were baptized.

With the big island as their home base, many of the Maga Christians began getting jobs on freighters and traveling two by two to other islands around them, sharing the gospel with other Maga people. In the previous three hundred years, there were only a handful of recorded Maga believers in that country, but today we have witnessed more than two thousand who have become disciples of Jesus. And that number is growing.

GOD IS MOVING AMONG MUSLIMS IN UNPRECEDENTED WAYS. MEN AND WOMEN WHO HAVE SACRIFICED THEIR LIVES FOR THE GOSPEL ARE NOW SEEING THE FRUIT OF THEIR LABORS. THROUGH PRAYER, SACRIFICE, AND LOVE, THE KINGDOM OF GOD IS ADVANCING.

The stories in this chapter are true, but some names have been changed and certain places have not been named in order to protect the safety of those involved.

CHAPTER 21

THE PASSION AND PURPOSE OF JESUS

I will build my church, and the gates of hell shall not prevail against it.

MATTHEW 16:18 (ESV)

Over two thousand years ago, Jesus stepped into our world with a passion and a purpose. Luke 4:18 records that in His first public message, He proclaimed these words from the prophecy of Isaiah:

"The spirit of the LORD is upon Me,
Because he anointed Me to preach the gospel to the poor.
He has sent Me to proclaim release to the captives,
And recovery of sight to the blind,
To set free those who are oppressed."

With that radical message, Jesus extended a radical invitation: "Follow Me." The invitation went out to an unexpected group of fishermen, tax collectors, harlots, and everyday, ordinary people. Through that invitation, He called disciples to be with Him. As they interacted with Him day by day, Jesus taught them about His Kingdom. He taught them how to live and to love in a different way. He modeled it with compassion and demonstrated it with power.

Perhaps the hardest thing for Jesus' followers to grasp was His teaching about His own death. He told them of His coming suffering and sacrifice, that He would die on a cross but He would rise again to make a way both for them and for the whole world to know the Father who created them. He told them He would build His church and the gates of hell would not prevail against it.

The Church Is Born

This newfound understanding of the Kingdom so transformed Jesus' followers, they were willing to give their own lives in order to carry His message all over the world.

Just before Jesus ascended into heaven, He told His followers, "You will receive power when the Holy Spirit has come upon you; and you shall be My witnesses both in Jerusalem, and in all Judea and Samaria, and even to the remotest part of the earth" (Acts 1:8). With faith, 120 of them gathered to pray and wait for Jesus' promise.

And then it happened just a few days later. Acts 2 says that the power of God came down so powerfully that it shook the place where they were meeting. Each person was filled with God's Spirit and went into the streets prophesying and speaking in the different languages of the people in the city. They told of the glory of God and His love for people. Peter jumped up and preached. Those listening were amazed, and they cried out, "What do we do to be saved?" Peter answered, "Repent and be baptized, and you will receive the gift of the Holy Spirit." And three thousand responded that day.

In one day the church was born. The ingathering of the people of God rightly living together in communion with Him and community with one another revealed His Kingdom on earth. The people who had said yes to the radical message of the Kingdom were beginning to experience its reality. In Acts

2:42-47, we see these believers gathering house to house, praying, studying the Word, experiencing a sense of equality and humility, seeing signs and wonders, feeling a sense of awe, and adding to their number day by day.

In those early days, as they lived out the values of the Kingdom before the whole city, they gained a reputation in Jerusalem. Acts 4:13 says, "Now as they observed the confidence of Peter and John and understood that they were uneducated and untrained men, they were amazed, and began to recognize them as having been with Jesus." The first church was known simply as a people who had been with Him. Day by day, they experienced Jesus and walked out His life together, and the world around them took notice.

Peter and the Acts 2 church were having a great time together in Jerusalem, so much so that they seemed to forget about Judea, Samaria, and the remotest parts of the earth—the very mission Jesus had called them to. But coming persecution would change that.

The church at Jerusalem was threatened, Christians were imprisoned, and some were even killed. The believers prayed about how to respond, and by the will and direction of God, some stayed in Jerusalem to see the church continue to grow, but others left. These did not flee Jerusalem simply to protect their own lives. They left because God was leading them.

As they went, they preached the same message they had heard in Jerusalem, the message of the Kingdom. And no matter where they traveled, they lived out the same Acts 2 church community they had lived in Jerusalem—house-to-house fellowship, worship, prayer, experiencing God, and seeing Him move powerfully in their midst. Because they faithfully carried the values of the Kingdom everywhere they went, the church continued to expand.

Throughout the book of Acts, we see churches established in Judea and Samaria, and new epicenters of church planting emerged in the cities of Antioch and Ephesus, reaching all of Asia Minor and Europe. Laborers were released, received back, refueled, and sent out again. The people they reached became on fire for God, embodying the values of the Kingdom, and corporately expressing those values to rightfully distribute the gospel. This is the way that the world will be won today, by the church being the church, carrying and imparting Kingdom values wherever we go.

For the original disciples, it was the simple values of knowing Jesus and making Him known that allowed them to endure persecution, to have joy in suffering, to experience power in their ministry, and to see the world changed. John said, "What was from the beginning, what we have heard, what we have seen with our eyes, what we have looked at and touched with our hands, concerning the Word of Life … we proclaim to you also, so that you too may have fellowship with us" (1 John 1:1-3). This church was alive with a people who had experienced the true God just as He had promised. Passion and purpose—this marked the church of the New Testament, and the world is longing to see that again.

In the spring of 2002, I was driving in my truck, listening to a Focus on the Family radio program. I realized that James Dobson was interviewing Dayna and Heather, the two Antioch missionaries who had been imprisoned in Afghanistan. Dr. Dobson was asking about their experience in prison. They were describing how they would hear the screams of Afghan men being beaten in the men's prison on the other side of the wall from their prison courtyard. They and four other foreign women they were imprisoned with would stand by the adjoining wall and pray for the beatings to stop. One day, in their prayers they were led to sing a song of intercession by Martin Smith called "There Is a Light." When they finished singing, they realized that the beatings had stopped and Jesus had intervened.

Dr. Dobson asked if they would mind singing that song, so they began, "There is a light that shines in the darkness … there is a light that shines in the darkness. His name is Jesus, His name is Jesus … He is the light of the world."

After they finished, it was quiet on the radio for a few seconds before Dr. Dobson said through tears, "Are you aware that when you say the name Jesus, you say it in a different way than many other people do? You say it in a way that shows deep, deep love and appreciation and compassion and respect. Are you aware of that?" He paused for a moment and then continued, "It shows through not just in the way you say Jesus' name but in what you have done with your lives."

Overcome with emotion, I turned off the radio and shouted, "You're right, James Dobson. And I know a thousand more just like them!"

Today, I walk with thousands of people who continue to have a passion for Jesus and His purposes in the earth, a people who are willing to give their lives and everything they are for the sake of the gospel.

May we all join together to be people of passion and purpose, believing that the church really can change the world.

EPILOGUE

As I'm sitting here writing, I will turn fifty years old in the next few days. As I reflect on all that God has done in my life, I can't help but be overwhelmed, not only with His great deeds but with the incredible people He has allowed our family to live among. When Laura and I first started this journey in 1987, we prayed a simple prayer: "God would you bring marvelous comrades to walk with us who fear Your name?"

As always, God has answered that prayer far above what we could ask or think. He has given us spiritual mothers and fathers who have encouraged us, spurred us on, and held us together in times of trial and struggle. He has given us beautiful friends to walk with and to experience life together in living radically for Jesus. He has given us sons and daughters in the faith who have taken the vision and values and, in many instances, are running faster and farther than we could have imagined. Those sons and daughters have become mothers and fathers as well, furthering the gospel for the glory of God. God has not just given us a purpose but a people and a family, too.

Our own kids are the joy of our lives. We could not be more proud of our son-in-law and daughter, Kyle and Abby Van Hecke; our daughter Lauren; and our sons, Caleb and Daniel. They have taken the values of the Kingdom and owned them in their own hearts, and we know they will truly go far beyond what Laura and I have experienced. They have been raised in this Antioch environment of radical love for Jesus and a commitment to His purposes. Laura and I both know that it was not just us who raised them, but the love and influence of this church family we call Antioch has also prepared them to go out to change the world themselves.

This past summer, Lauren and Caleb, now college students, were with a group of friends planting a new church among students and young professionals in Ulaanbaatar, the capital city of Mongolia. They sent me a picture of themselves with three friends, Daniel Mueller, Joshua Franzen, and Hannah Franzen. These young adults all grew up in families who have served alongside us for twenty plus years. The caption under the photo, which captured big smiles of excitement on their faces, read "The Next Generation." Overcome with emotion, I realized that this has always been the goal: not that Laura and I and a few friends would do something significant in our little bit of time here on earth, but that we would see our own children—and their children and generations of young people to follow—carrying on this great call to see Jesus glorified and this world transformed.

ACKNOWLEDGEMENTS

The hardest part about writing a book about the Antioch family is the limitation of time and space. There are so many more stories that could be told and so many more names that could be mentioned. I know, and most importantly God knows, how much love and sacrifice has been given and lived out so these Kingdom stories could be a testimony to others. Laura and I love and value each of you so much and are so thankful for you. These stories of faith are a part of all of us, and without each of you it would never be complete.

On a project of this magnitude, there are always those who have helped to bring it to completion. I want to specifically thank my long-time assistant and co-laborer, Mary Greenwald. Your hours of prayer, love, and diligence to work by my side has made this possible. I want to thank Jeff Abshire and Drew Steadman for their long hours of review and feedback, counseling, and editing along the way. Thank you for always having my back and truly being brothers in seeing this project completed. I also want to thank Kendra Pulliam and Kyle Rogers. Your creativity and attention to detail is a gift to all of us.

I am also grateful for Clear Day Publishing and my brother and sister-in-law, David and Melinda Seibert, who have always believed in us, supported us, and worked tirelessly to make sure this project was finished with excellence. A special thanks to the great group of investors and friends behind the scenes who have financially made a way for us all.

I want to acknowledge that God has given us many spiritual mothers and fathers whose contributions alone could fill a book. In the past two years, three of those fathers went to be with Jesus: Ben Loring, Ron Allison, and Darrell Atwood. Each of these men loved and supported Laura and me and our whole movement by believing in us and laying down their lives for us all. One of those fathers, Darrell Atwood, became like a surrogate father to Laura and me, always loving us, caring for us and believing in us. His love, prayers, and wisdom laid a foundation for where we are today. He would often say, "Jimmy, God has answered our prayers above and beyond. It is always what I prayed I would see in my lifetime." Darrell, as well as Ron and Ben, will forever be in the fabric of who we are and who God has called us to be.

Lastly, how can I not stop again and acknowledge our Lord Jesus, the One who calls us, keeps us, and sustains us? Thank You, Jesus, that Your story never ends in each of our lives until we stand face to face with You.

ANTIOCH CHURCHES

Antioch Community Church – Waco, TX

antiochcc.com | Facebook: AntiochWaco | Twitter: Antioch_Waco

---

Antioch International Movement of Churches

The Antioch International Movement of Churches is a group of churches connected through the power and work of the Holy Spirit and by a desire to love God, love one another, and love those who do not know Jesus.

Whether in Waco, around the U.S., or in the most remote parts of the earth, we believe a local church committed to evangelism and discipleship can change the world.

U.S. CHURCHES AS OF SPRING 2014

Ann Arbor, MI | **Antioch Community Church** | antiocha2.org

Baton Rouge, LA | **Antioch Community Church** | antiochbr.com

Belton, TX | **Antioch Community Church** | antiochbelton.org

Beverly, MA | **The Harbor** | the-harbor.net

Boston, MA | **Community of Faith Christian Fellowship** | cfcfboston.org

College Station, TX | **Antioch Community Church** | antiochcs.org

Dallas, TX | **Antioch Community Church** | antiochdallas.org

Edmonds, WA | **Mosaic Community Church** | mosaic-edmonds.org

Fort Collins, CO | **Antioch Community Church** | antiochfc.org

Fort Worth, TX | **Christ Fellowship** | christfellowship.org

Fullerton, CA | **Antioch Community Church** | antiochfullerton.com

Houston, TX | **Antioch Community Church** | antiochhouston.com

Knoxville, TN | **Antioch Community Church** | antiochknox.org

Lawrence, KS | **Antioch Community Church** | antiochlawrence.org

Lincoln Heights, CA | **Epicentre Church** | epicentrechurch.org

Norman, OK | **Antioch Community Church** | antiochnorman.com

Omaha, NE | **Waypoint Church** | waypointomaha.com

Orlando, FL | **Antioch Community Church** | antiochorlando.com

Pasadena, CA | **Epicentre Church** | epicentrechurch.org

Raleigh, NC | **Antioch Community Church** | antiochraleigh.com

San Diego, CA | **All Peoples Church** | allpeopleschurch.org

Seattle, WA | **Mosaic Community Church** | mosaic-seattle.org

Tempe, AZ | **Antioch Community Church** | antiochtempe.org

Waco, TX | **Antioch Community Church** | antiochcc.com

Waltham, MA | **The River Church** | theriverwaltham.org

Wheaton, IL | **Antioch Community Church** | acc-w.org

West Los Angeles, CA | **Epicentre West LA** | epicentrewestla.org

INTERNATIONAL CHURCH PLANT TEAMS

Africa	**East Asia**	**Middle East**	**South America**
NW Africa	India	Indigo	Peru
Northern Africa	Northern India	Middle East 1	Brazil
South Africa	Everest	Dubai	
Cameroon	Japan		**Europe**
Namibia	Mongolia	**South Asia**	Brussels
Uganda	Russia		England
	Sri Lanka	**Latin America**	Italy
Central Asia	Thailand	Haiti	Portugal
	NK		Scotland

Exact locations have been omitted or coded for the security of our workers.

ABOUT THE AUTHOR

Jimmy Seibert is the senior pastor of Antioch Community Church in Waco, Texas, as well as the founder and president of Antioch Ministries International (AMI). He has served the Antioch church in that role since its establishment in 1999.

Jimmy is passionate about loving God and making Him known in all the earth. He and his wife, Laura, have been involved in training and sending out church planters for more than twenty-six years, seeing hundreds of Christians go to the mission field. Their desire is to see the local church own the vision of establishing churches throughout the earth.

Throughout their humble journey of simple devotion and obedience, Jimmy, Laura, and those who have served with them at Antioch have been overwhelmed by the Lord's faithfulness, goodness, and power. Under their leadership, Antioch Community Church has grown and impacted Waco, Texas, and planted churches in the U.S. and around the world.

Jimmy and his wife, Laura, have been married for twenty-seven years. Their children include their daughter Abby and her husband, Kyle Van Hecke, daughter Lauren, and two sons, Caleb, and Daniel.

antiochcc.com/jimmyseibert | Twitter: @Jimmy_Seibert

Live Worship Album by

ⒶANTIOCHLIVE

Available on iTunes, Amazon
and at ClearDayWorship.com

facebook.com/antiochlive
Antiochcc.com
ClearDayWorship.com